Ove Korsgaard

Peoplehood

in the Nordic World

Aarhus University Press / The University of Wisconsin Press

The Nordic World
Peoplehood in the Nordic World
© Ove Korsgaard 2022

Cover, layout, and typesetting:
Camilla Jørgensen, Trefold
Cover photograph: Morten Holtum
Translation: Heidi Flegal
Copy editor: Mia Gaudern
Acquisitions editors: Amber Rose Cederström
and Karina Bell Ottosen
This book is typeset in FS Ostro and printed
on Munken Lynx 130 g
Printed by Narayana Press, Denmark
Printed in Denmark 2022

ISBN 978 87 7219 725 8
ISBN 978 0 299 33904 3

This book is available in a digital edition

Library of Congress Cataloging-in-Publication
data is available

Published with the generous support of the
Aarhus University Research Foundation,
the Carlsberg Foundation and the Nordic
Council of Ministers

The Nordic World series is copublished by
Aarhus University Press and the University
of Wisconsin Press

Aarhus University Press
aarhusuniversitypress.dk

The University of Wisconsin Press
uwpress.wisc.edu

PEER
REVIEWED

MIX
Paper
FSC FSC® C010651

Contents

Chapter 1

Introduction

The word "people" represents one of the most complex and conflict-ridden concepts in the English language, and in many other languages as well. It is complex because it has many and diverse meanings, and it is conflict-ridden because the word evokes very different associations for different people: highly positive for some, extremely negative for others. This word can be used to unite individuals and to divide groups, and to propagandize in favor of either democracy or dictatorship. People is therefore a very fluid concept, often used strategically, and its semantic content is wide open. Put simply, both people and peoplehood are in a constant state of creation and re-creation.

This book deals with the concept of peoplehood, which one acknowledged definition, from Merriam-Webster, describes as "the quality or state of constituting a people" and as "the awareness of the underlying unity that makes the individual a part of a people". More specifically, it discusses the significance that peoplehood has for nation building in the Nordic countries, particularly the Scandinavian countries. Here, Denmark will serve as my main example in illustrating the significance of peoplehood as a concept, supplemented with examples from Norway and Sweden. To shed light on the characteristic Nordic brand of nation building, the book also takes a more sweeping view across the last 500 years of European history.

The main part of the book discusses key structural components shared by three of the Nordics – the Scandinavian countries Denmark, Norway, and Sweden – that were not created during one specific historical period, but stretched across several. Three periods are absolutely crucial: (a) the Reformation in the early 1500s; (b) the agrarian movement and, later, the labor movement in the second half of the 1800s and the first half of the 1900s; and (c) the development of the welfare state from the 1930s up to the present.

State building and nation building

Modern political theory differentiates between nation building and state building. The difference, in a nutshell, is that a "state" is a legal institution and is linked to a certain territory – you can literally take a walk in the state – whereas a "nation" is based on an idea. In the elegant wording of the Irish-American anthropologist Benedict Anderson, a nation is an imagined community. The members of even the tiniest nation would never know most of the other members, yet in the mind of each one an idea has developed about the things they have in common (Anderson 1983).

Like Benedict Anderson, the American political philosopher Francis Fukuyama distinguishes between state and nation:

> State building refers to the creation of tangible institutions – armies, police, bureaucracies, ministries, and the like. (...) Nation building, by contrast, is the creation of a sense of national identity to which individuals will be loyal, an identity that will supersede their loyalty to tribes, villages, regions, and ethnic

8

groups. Nation building in contrast to state building requires the creation of intangible things like national traditions, symbols, shared historical memories, and common cultural points of reference. National identities can be created by states through their policies on language, religion, and education. But they are often established from the bottom up by poets, philosophers, religious leaders, novelists, musicians, and other individuals with no direct access to political power. (Fukuyama 2014: 285)

Fukuyama sees Denmark as an especially interesting case in point "because a strong national identity emerged as the result of a bottom-up process in a country that was liberal and democratizing" (Fukuyama 2015: 42). This bottom-up process is intimately connected to the significance that the rural class had for the development of a Danish national identity, which is also true for Norway and Sweden.

However, it is important to bear in mind that for several centuries religion played a pivotal role in building a shared religious identity in both Sweden and what was then the dual monarchy of Denmark-Norway. This process was decidedly top-down, not bottom-up, and Martin Luther (1483–1546) was an essential figure in it. His religious ideas became central to state building and identity construction in the Nordics. Protestantism legitimized the organization of "territorial states", a collective term used for the north German and Nordic kingdoms, and princely states (or principalities), which rose to prominence in the 1500s and replaced the more loosely organized states of the Middle Ages.

Centuries later, the French Revolution of 1789 brought not only a new type of government – democracy – but also a new type of state: the nation-state. The result was a momentous paradigm shift in the ideological foundation of the state, from a basis of shared religious identity to one of shared national identity. In his 2015 article "Icon of Nationalism", the British nationalism researcher Anthony D. Smith pointed out the demands of this new type of nation building:

> This task requires leaders who will to some extent embody the nation's charisma and, for that reason, are in a position to mobilize 'the people' not just for resistance to an external oppressor but also, and more important, to rediscover themselves, their inner strength and 'true' identity. That, in turn, requires that they engage in vernacular education, or re-education, as the case may be, a process of turning inward to search for the distinctive elements and authentic qualities of 'the people' in order to remake them as citizens of a unique and charismatic culture community. (Smith 2015: 59)

Smith calls these leaders "national educators" and identifies the Swiss philosopher Jean-Jacques Rousseau and the German scholar of culture and language Johann Gottfried von Herder as pioneers in this field, thanks to their focus on "national self-expression, self-realization, and self-determination" (Smith 2015: 60). He also mentions a number of other individuals who served as national educators in their respective countries. These include the American writer and philosopher Ralph Waldo Emerson, the French historian Jules Michelet, and the Czech politician and philosopher Tomáš Masaryk. In a Danish context, Smith has identified an example that personifies such decisive influence on a country's national identity:

> The outstanding case is that of the theologian Nikolaj Grundtvig in Denmark. Almost single-handedly Grundtvig changed the moral, social, and educa-

tional content of subsequent Danish politics. (...) Not only did he recommend freedom of association in worship, albeit within the Lutheran sphere, but he also inspired a network of 'Folk High Schools', based on his liberal philosophy. (Smith 2015: 69)

N. F. S. Grundtvig,[1] who lived from 1783 to 1872, was an enormously proliferous writer, poet, historian, theologian, pastor, politician, and pedagogical thinker. During his long and active life, he went from being a marginal, controversial voice on the fringes of Danish society to becoming a founding father of and a key figure in a nationwide cultural and social movement – "Grundtvigianism" – supported by large parts of the country's rural population. Grundtvig is a remarkable example of a national educator who hugely influenced a country's self-understanding and sense of peoplehood, and therefore he will be a recurring figure throughout this book.

Anthony D. Smith regards the Norwegian writer and poet Henrik Wergeland, who lived from 1808 to 1845, as Norway's national educator par excellence. A similarly prominent Swedish educator was the historian and writer Erik Gustaf Geijer, who lived from 1783 to 1847. Both were driving forces behind the developments that put farmers and peasants at the very core of the people in their respective countries.

Although Grundtvig, Wergeland, and Geijer are iconic names, and rightly so, they were obviously not alone in making important contributions to nation building in Denmark, Norway, and Sweden. In this book I will mainly focus on Denmark, my own country and the one whose history I know best, but I will also highlight a number of prominent figures from the other two Scandinavian countries.

The book's basic premise is that what is often called "the Nordic way of life" – a phrase broadly applied to soci-

1. In Denmark he is simply referred to by his last name, although sometimes his initials (for Nikolaj Frederik Severin) are included

Nicolai Frederik Severin Grundtvig (1783–1872) was a Danish poet, pastor, historian, politician, and educator of the people. Grundtvig is without doubt the single individual who has had the greatest influence on the formation of the Danish nation. Few can match the renown he would later gain as a nation builder. © Lennart Larsen / Det Nationalhistoriske Museum på Frederiksborg Slot

etal models, politics, cultural features, and ways of living - came into being through two distinct but closely linked historical processes: state building and nation building. The former is primarily seen as the result of a political process, the latter as the result of a formative-educational and identity-generating process. The main topic in focus throughout the book is the importance that education and "popular enlightenment" held for nation building.

Chapter 2

Father and people

Folk exists as an ancient concept in most languages in the Nordic region.[2] In a dictionary of old Danish, entitled *Ordbog til det ældre danske Sprog 1300–1700*, *folk* ("people") is defined as family or kin, roughly: "my people and father's house, with fathers, relatives, and mothers; my earliest people, great-great grandfather, and great-grandfather."[3] In a dictionary of old Norwegian, entitled *Ordbog over det gamle norske Sprog*, the entry *folk* is similarly defined as "housefolk, those persons who are in one's house, belonging to one's household", and also as "blood-related persons, persons who belong to one's family or ancestral line".[4] Neither in the old Danish nor the old Dano-Norwegian written language is the word *folk* associated with the concept of the nation or nationhood.

Throughout history the household has been one of the most ubiquitous and continuous phenomena in human activity. The Greek word for household is *oikos*; it is the root of modern words like *eco*nomy and *eco*logy, which relate to the household. An *oikos* was a house(hold), the members of which were led by a father. In antiquity, society was based on a complementary division into the spheres of *oikos* and *polis*, and this division runs through European political philosophy, from Aristotle to Cicero to

Luther and all the way up to Rousseau. Aristotle shows in the introduction to his work *A Treatise on Government* that he clearly regarded the *oikos* as the fundamental building block of the *polis*, or Greek city-state, the most well known of which was Athens. According to this philosophy, the smallest functional unit in society is not the individual but the household, meaning that the body of a society consists of a certain number of households.

Before the rise of modern society, the household was the most important unit of production, reproduction, organization, and management. A Scandinavian household was led by a *husbond* ("husband"), who was the master of the house. The designation *husbond* was applied equally to all heads of households (who were invariably male), whether the master of the house was a tailor, a count, or a king. What these three shared was their status as "housemaster", even though their individual households were not of equal rank. The structure of society was comparable to a set of nested boxes, where small households would be part of a larger household, which in turn was part of an even larger household, and so on – the very highest housemaster being the Lord God, who held the power to make decisions about everyone's lives. During Denmark's age of absolute monarchy (from 1660 to 1848), the king held and wielded power "by the grace of God," implying that God had delegated power to the monarch, who could, in turn, delegate parts of his power to the many masters ranking lower, and so on down through the system.

The qualities we now attribute to the word "state" were formerly attributed to the household or house, as in "the royal household", "a princely house", or "a noble house". [5] In fact, up until 1789, Europe, including the Nordic region, was organized not into nation-states but into principalities and royal houses, each consisting of a certain number of households.

3. Otto Kalkar, *Ordbog til det ældre danske Sprog* (Thieles Forlag 1981-1918). The entry written in old Danish reads: "mit folck og faders huus, med fædre, slegt og mødre, min første folkefær, tip-fader, oldermand"

4. Johan Frizner, *Ordbog over Det gamle norske Sprog* (Den norske Forlagsforening 1886). The entry written in old Dano-Norwegian reads: "Husfolk, de Mennesker, som ere i ens Hus, hører til ens Husholdning," and "beslægtede Mennesker, Personer som tilhøre ens Slægt eller Ætt"

5. This meaning of the word "house" lives on today, for instance in certain names of large companies and fashion brands

The two central institutions were the House of the King and the House of the Lord, with the throne and the altar serving as the two most important symbols in Danish class-based society. In accordance with the doctrine *Cuius Regio, Eius Religio* (literally: "whose realm, their religion," as in "the ruler's religion shall rule"), only the king's faith was permitted within the state. "A Christian king," declared Bishop Hans Wandal at the anointing of Christian V of Denmark in 1671, "must not tolerate anyone in his lands who does not keep to the proper teaching, and must not permit the Devil and the heretics to sow the tares [weeds] in God's own field" (Historiegruppen 1950: 352).

Although the concept of the *fædreland* (fatherland), can be traced far back in history, up until the 1700s it played an inferior role compared to the Crown and the Church. As the Danish historian Harald Ilsøe put it in a work on the history of Danish identity: "In the ideological alliance between the power of the king and the teachings of Luther, in principle the concept of 'fatherland' held no meaning" (Ilsøe 1991: 33). In the prescribed prayer in every church service, for instance, the congregation would pray only for the preservation of the king and his family, and not for anyone else. Even the prescribed prayers of supplication and thanksgiving for a country's progress and victory in war mainly focused on the monarch and his armed forces.

The Danish king's house included a variety of fatherlands, although this did not mean or imply that their populations were regarded as "foreign". In the words of a Danish nobleman, Grunde Rosenkrantz, reported in 1665: "As for those who originate from Holstein and Schleswig and Norway, I do not call them foreign. They do not have the same fatherland, but they do have the same master and are bound to us by ties of kinship" (Ilsøe 1991: 28). The king was the joint master of the house, and he not only personified the kinship among those living in the kingdom but also determined their religious faith and beliefs.

In *Danske Lov*, the "Danish law" adopted in 1683, and also in the nearly identical *Norske Lov*, the "Norwegian law" adopted in 1687, the power of the king is clearly set out in the preamble. The king must be honored as the "highest head" or supreme ruler on Earth. When, in the law, the king marks out the boundaries of his territory, this is meant as a delineation addressed to the housemasters of the kingdom. The reason is that a housemaster held a special legal position compared to other groups in society, referred to as househands, people, and servants.

Before the adoption of the new Danish Constitution in 1849, Denmark was still a rank- and class-based society, although the previously very rigid system had begun to soften somewhat. Danish society was hierarchically organized, with the Crown atop the pyramid. Beneath this, a simplified model would show four classes (historically called "estates") in descending order, each with its own functions and its particular rights and obligations. Below the king ranked the nobility, followed by the clergy. These we can call class I and class II, and they were especially privileged and perceived themselves as free – unlike class III and class IV, which were the citizenry and the peasantry, respectively.

In Denmark and other similar class-based societies, the nobility and the clergy did not see themselves as part of the people. The aristocratic and religious elite represented the nation, according to the French political philosopher Charles de Montesquieu: "During the first two French princely houses, the nation was often united, i.e. the nobility and bishops. The people were not taken into account" (Zernatto 1944: 361ff.). By the same token, the Danish pastor Hans Peter Kofoed-Hansen, whose book *Et Folk – Folket* ("*A people – the people*") appeared in 1869, wrote that as far back as one can see historically, "the no-

16

Martin Luther (1483-1546) was a German theologian and a key figure in the Reformation, which changed the Church's rituals and teachings. Protestantism indisputably exerted an influence on the Nordic mentality through its uncompromising politics of identity formation, which for more than 350 years required virtually everyone in the region to learn Luther's *Small Catechism* by heart. © PRISMA ARCHIVO / Alamy Stock

bility and the clerics themselves would most respectfully decline the honor of being counted as part of 'the people'" (Kofoed-Hansen 1869: 258). The noblemen and clerics made up the nation; the farmers and peasants made up the people.

In all of the Nordic societies, the word for "people" was primarily used to denote the lower classes. The law was not equal for all, as the different classes had different rights and obligations. For instance, the peasants were the only class that had to serve as soldiers.

The sovereignty of father and master

The Reformation in the early 1500s played an important role in the evolution of the Nordic societies and ways of life. In Sweden, King Gustav Vasa implemented the Reformation in 1527, and in the twin kingdom comprising Denmark and Norway the Reformation was officially implemented in 1536.

Luther was not concerned with civil liberties. On the contrary, he believed it obvious that one could not transfer political power to the people, an idea he often criticized vehemently. This put his thinking in line with that of the German nobility, who had no interest in supporting German nationalism or the democratic overtones this carried. Guardianship was, and would remain, a fundamental pillar of Luther's political and didactic thinking. Throughout the Nordic countries, Luther's educational philosophy became immensely important in shaping mentality and identity, as his *Small Catechism* assumed the status of a mandatory handbook in civic instruction for children and young people – retaining this status for more than 350 years.

Luther wrote his *Small Catechism* in 1529, with the aim of teaching readers how to live in a society controlled by fathers, masters, and guardians. The book was written as an aid to the "housefather" or master of the household, whose task it was to teach the members of his household the basic principles of Christianity. An introductory comment to each new section states that the following is what "a father should present (...) to his household" (Smith 1994), namely the Ten Commandments, the Creed, the Lord's Prayer, and so forth. Luther regards the fourth commandment, *Thou shalt honor thy father and thy mother*, as crucial.

Luther did not use the words "father" and "mother" only about children's biological parents, but also about authority figures in general. The fourth commandment therefore also contains a requirement to show obedience to public officials.

The sovereignty of the father is at the very crux of Luther's social philosophy and his theology. In his eyes, a public official as father "is not one of a single family, but of as many people as he has tenants, citizens, or subjects. For through them, as through our parents, God gives to us food, house and home, protection and security." Luther concludes that the fourth commandment reveals that there are three kinds of secular fathers: those of "the blood", "the household", and "the country". Beyond and set apart from these, he identifies a fourth kind: "the spiritual fathers", meaning the evangelical pastors whose task it is to refer their children to God the Father (Bente & Dau 1921).

With the Reformation implemented and use of the printing press becoming ever more widespread, the Bible was translated into Danish and Swedish, greatly influencing the development of languages across the Nordic region. As the Canadian media philosopher Marshall McLuhan was already pointing out around the mid-1960s: "Political unification of populations by means of vernacular and language groupings was unthinkable before printing turned each vernacular into an extensive mass medium" (McLuhan 1964). According to McLuhan, written language was a precondition for the development of nationalism in its modern form.

Peoplehood and nation

Not until the 1700s did European political philosophy really break with the notion, which harked back to antiquity, that a society consists of two spheres: *oikos* and *polis*. The new thinking of the 1700s came to divide society into three spheres: the state, the market, and civil society. In parallel with this process the scope of the household narrowed down to the home, meaning the framework surrounding a nuclear family. At the same time the concept of the nation was expanded to include "the people" as well.

In England the two concepts of people and nation began to converge during the 1600s and 1700s. The shift originated with the Puritans, a group who, during the English Civil War of 1642–1649, developed the earliest ideas

19

of "the people" being the most powerful component in a society (Greenfeld 1992: 506). This is clearly seen, for instance, in a manifesto promulgated by the English Puritans on January 4, 1649: "That the people are, under God, the original of all just power" and "that the Commons of England, in Parliament assembled, being chosen by and representing the people, have the supreme power in this nation" (Schuyler 1929: 82).

As phrased by the Danish historian Laurids Engelstoft in his work from 1808 entitled *Tanker om National-opdragelsen* ("Thoughts on National Upbringing"): "To quite some extent, England was the first and, for many years, the only nation which, with unprejudiced impartiality, opened the temple of honor to all classes" (Engelstoft 1808: 266) – meaning that the people were let in too. Engelstoft believed that Denmark ought to do the same, since broadening the concept of the nation would strengthen Danish society's internal cohesion. He believed that the more privileges of rank and class are broken down, "the more the inner power of society increases" (Engelstoft 1808: 182).

A similar view relating to the developments in England is presented by the American historian of ideas Leah Greenfeld in her book *Nationalism* from 1992. Here, she argues that the first expressions of modern nationalism and national feelings can be identified in England in the early 1600s. According to Greenfeld, the political process in England led to a semantic transformation of the concepts of "people" and "nation": "This semantic transformation signaled the emergence of the first nation in the world, in the sense in which the word is understood today, and launched the era of nationalism" (Greenfeld 1992: 6).

Nevertheless, it was only with the French Revolution in 1789 that the developments in England could be clearly explained and manifested. In France the king was removed as the head and father in favor of a notion of a so-

Gustav Vasa, or King Gustav I of Sweden (1496-1560), reigned from 1523 to 1560, during which time he liberated his country from Danish dominance and made its monarchy hereditary. The Reformation was also introduced in Sweden during his reign, in 1527, but the transition was slow, only coming to an end with the Uppsala Synod in 1593. © History and Art Collection / Alamy Stock

cial order based on democratic and national brotherhood, as expressed in the revolutionary slogan: "*Liberté, égalité, fraternité*" – "freedom, equality, and brotherhood."

The shift away from the firm connection between "people and father" towards the association of "people and nation" is reflected in the Nordic region's languages. A large number of older compound words including *folke-* or *-folk* fell out of use during the 1800s, but at the same time new words of this type were continuously entering the language.

These new words fell into three categories, representing three different meanings and perceptions of the concept of *folk*: one political, one cultural, and one social (that is, a class concept). Note that the second of these is closely linked to the English culture-related use of word "folk", as in folk songs and folklore.

The Greek concepts of *demos, ethnos* and *pléthos* form the linguistic background for the political, cultural and social understanding of the concept of people, respectively.

Taking a somewhat simplified approach, we can identify these three concepts by means of political thinkers such as Jean-Jacques Rousseau, Johann Gottfried von Herder, and Karl Marx and Friedrich Engels. Although immensely different, they all imbue the concepts "people" and "nation" with new meaning. Rousseau sees people as a political concept; Herder sees it as a linguistic and cultural concept; and Marx and Engels see it as a social concept. These three definitions are all modern in the sense that they distance themselves from the old understanding of people as individuals or groups who are subordinated to, or subjects of, a master.

Here, it is crucial to distinguish between people as subordinates and people as subjects. In a rank-based society, "the people" are not only legally defined as subordinates; many also consider *themselves* as subordinated to others. But "the people" who define themselves as a lower class do not accept the power structures, and struggle to change them. In other words, the lower class strives to become sovereign, meaning: it strives to capture the right to speak on behalf of the nation. This is precisely what Marx and Engels were encouraging the proletariat or working class to do in 1848. In the English version of *The Manifesto of the Communist Party*, edited by "Fredrick Engels" himself, they underline this point, touched on above: "Since the proletariat must first of all acquire political supremacy, must rise to be the leading class of the nation, must constitute itself the nation, it is, so far, itself national, though not in the bourgeois sense of the word" (Moore 1888).

Chapter 3.

Establishing democracies and nation-states

"We the People of the United States." This line opens the preamble of the American Constitution, written and adopted in 1787, but it also contains an unresolved question: Who are "we"? Who makes up the people behind the people's government?

The word "people" lies at the core of the concept of democracy, a term built from the two Greek words *demos* and *kratia* meaning, respectively, "people" and "rule". Democracy therefore implicitly claims that there is a people who governs. There are many theories about the nature of the state and democratic rule, but when it comes to defining the nature of "the people who rule", all we have are what could be called shadow theories.

One thinker who has spotlighted the difficulties of identifying the people underlying a democracy is the American democracy scholar Robert A. Dahl. In his book *Democracy and Its Critics* (1991), he phrases this theoretical question as follows: "If democracy means government by the people, what constitutes 'a people'? There may be no problem in the whole domain of democratic theory and practice more intractable than the one posed by this innocent-seeming question" (Dahl 1991: 116).

Francis Fukuyama, introduced in Chaper 1, has also pointed out that neither the American Constitution nor the French Declaration of the Rights of Man and of the Citizen, from 1789, stipulates

> who the people are, or on what basis individuals are to be included in the national community. The silence in the American Constitution raises some important questions: Where does national identity come from in the first place, and how is it defined? What makes for a 'people' whose sovereignty is the basis for democratic choice?

For instance, the American Constitution provided no answer as to why, later, the border between the United States and Mexico was laid out to follow the course of the Rio Grande, nor did the French Declaration make any statement about whether the Alsace/Elsass region ought to belong to France or to Germany (Fukuyama 2018: 133ff.).

When, on June 20, 1789, the body of middle-class revolutionaries in Paris declared itself the National Constituent Assembly, it claimed to represent the entire French people - the nation - and not just a single class or community. However, carrying out the political transformation process from class to nation and applying this as a constituting principle of society turned out to be highly contentious and extremely bloody. In 1793-1794 the French Revolution developed into a reign of terror under the rule of a group called the Society of Jacobins, infamously led by Maximilien Robespierre. Beginning in 1792, revolutionary France engaged in a number of wars that gradually came to involve the whole of Europe, including the Nordic countries. Then, in 1799, Napoleon Bonaparte carried out a coup d'état, assuming power and subsequently transforming France into an empire, installing himself as Emperor. The wars continued through 1804, the year of Napoleon's crowning, and only ended with his final defeat at Waterloo in 1815, followed by the Congress of Vienna that same year.

The Napoleonic Wars wiped several hundred princely and royal houses off the maps of Europe. In the years that followed, the general opinion was that small states were no longer meaningful, as they could not form the basis of independent nation-states. Thus, to avoid being gobbled up by larger states – as Poland had been in the late 1700s by Russia, Prussia, and Austria – small states had best join forces with nearby kindred states if they wanted to survive.

The Napoleonic Wars also reshaped the Nordic region. When Russia seized Finland from Sweden in 1809, the Swedish state was thrown into turmoil, leading to the appointment of Jean-Baptiste Bernadotte, Napoleonic Marshal of France, as the crown prince of Sweden under the name of Karl Johan. Moreover, after the British bombardment of Copenhagen in 1807, Denmark officially decided to side with France in the conflict (in which it had originally sought to stay neutral). This decision ended up dragging the Dano-Norwegian state down with Napoleon when he fell. As a result of the peace negotiated in the Treaty of Kiel, signed on January 14, 1814, Denmark was obliged to give up Norway to Swedish rule – after 434 years as a "dual monarchy" or twin state, which had Copenhagen as its administrative capital.

In connection with Norway's secession from the kingdom of Denmark, on May 17, 1814, the newly independent country adopted what is known as the Eidsvoll Constitution, named after the estate where it was signed. By contemporary standards this constitution was quite a remarkable manifestation of the Enlightenment's ideas of popular sovereignty, human rights, and the sharing of power. The Eidsvoll Constitution is the oldest constitution in Europe that is still in force.

Even after 1814 the Danish monarchy remained multinational and multilingual, as a kingdom consisting (until the border war of 1864) of two central parts, three peripheral parts, and several small enclaves around the world. The central parts were Denmark itself, which consisted of the main archipelago (around Zealand and Funen) and the Jutland peninsula down to the Kongeå river, and the duchies of Schleswig and Holstein (including Lauenburg). The peripheral parts consisted of the islands in the north Atlantic that made up Iceland, the Faroe Islands, and Greenland. In addition, Denmark had several small overseas colonies: the Danish West Indies (after 1917, the US Virgin Islands in the Caribbean), Tranquebar (in India), and the Danish Gold Coast colony (in modern-day Ghana). Clearly, the wider kingdom encompassed a variety of ethnic peoples who spoke many different languages: Danish, Norwegian, Low German, Icelandic, Faroese, Greenlandic, and numerous local languages. The two largest languages, however, were Danish and Low German. Those living in Holstein and Lauenburg spoke Low German; in Schleswig about half the population spoke Danish and the other half Low German. Across Jutland and the Danish archipelago most of the population spoke Danish (many with distinct dialects), while both Danish and German were heard in the capital of Copenhagen.

In 1830 another revolution broke out in Paris. King Charles X was cast out, and a new king, Louis Philippe, was elected on the promise of reform. Belgium seceded from the Netherlands and, the following year, adopted a democratic constitution. Greece, Poland, and Italy all saw the rise of revolutionary movements fighting for national independence. The waves of change washing across Europe also broke on the shores of the multinational

26

Danish state. An administrative officer in the Schleswig-Holstein region, Uwe Jens Lornsen, wrote a 12-page call to arms, publicly raising the question of the legal national status of Schleswig. In this piece Lornsen advocated the establishment of a national assembly and an independent constitution, with joint parliamentary representation for the two duchies of Schleswig and Holstein – and for his efforts he was arrested and sentenced to a year in prison.

In 1830 the German Confederation, which consisted of 38 German states, also began to strongly advocate an advisory assembly for Holstein, which itself was a member of the German Confederation, a fact that caused continual unrest. It was therefore under a certain amount of coercion that the Danish king, Frederik VI, who was also the Duke of Holstein, announced the following year that four advisory assemblies would be established, respectively, in Holstein, Schleswig, Northern Jutland, and the Islands. The composition of these assemblies was published in 1834, and the first meeting was held in 1835.

The coercive aspect involved in installing these advisory assemblies was twofold. Not only was the king averse to such proto-democratic institutions, he was also afraid of national movements making their mark in the German lands and across the Danish kingdom. If these movements gained too much momentum, it might catastrophically undermine the multinational and multilingual nature of the Danish kingdom. The truly disquieting question was what position the German-speaking part of the kingdom's population would take once the two German advisory assemblies got down to work.

N. F. S. Grundtvig, who is sometimes called the ultimate philosopher of Danishness, feared the kind of nationalism that was developing in the German-speaking areas. This trend was put into words by a number of national revolutionary thinkers such as the writer and scholar E. M. Arndt and the physical education pioneer F. L. *"Turn-*

vater" ("father of gymnastics") Jahn. In his book *Deutsches Volkstum* ("German peoplehood") from 1810, Jahn referred to the status of the Danish people as connected or "adjunct" to the Germans. His preface to the book pays tribute to Prussia as "the trunk of the German tree", imagining that its branches will stretch beneficially across Europe: "When Germany is united under Prussian leadership, it will forever create peace in Europe and become the guardian angel of humanity" (Nielsen 1971: 147).

In 1838, Grundtvig (born in 1783) gave a series of lectures on developments in Europe during his own lifetime. In one of these he reproached *Turnvater* Jahn for instilling in young people a "limitless national pride and deep scorn for all things foreign."[6] In Grundtvig's view, the Danish understanding of *folk* and *folkelig* (the people, and popular) was something quite different; it was open towards that which was foreign. This understanding, he claimed, did not resonate with the Germans, "since they have long held the assumption that *Germanness* and *universal humanity* are but two names for the same idea". In short, his critique of the Germans was that they made Germanness the only quality worth striving for, and equated the particular with the universal.

In Grundtvig's interpretation, this conceptual equation of particular and universal was the ideological backdrop for the expansive nature of German nationalism. He therefore found it extremely fortunate for Europe that Germany was divided into many smaller states. As he saw it, the unification of German lands would lead to the rise of a "monstrous German war machine" and result in a highly aggressive superpower. A German Confederation under the leadership of a Prussian state ready for war would, he believed, be just as detrimental to Germany as to the rest of Europe. The tyrannical regime exercised across Europe by the French Napoleon would pale in comparison to "a *German* Emperor Napoleon" who would arise if Germany

6. Most of the Grundtvig quotes appearing in English in this and subsequent chapters have been translated by Edward Broadbridge for the book *The Common Good. N.F.S. Grundtvig as Politician and Contemporary Historian*, edited by Edward Brodbridge and Ove Korsgaard (Aarhus University Press 2019), with Grundtvig's emphasis [pp. 45, n. 67; 46, n. 69; 47, n. 73; 46; 253; 344; 348; 247; 337; 338; 38; 230; 297; 287; 301]. Others have been translated or paraphrased for the purposes of this book by its author and translator

were to be united. And if that eventually happened, it would pose an enormous security risk, if not an existential threat, to Denmark. In hindsight, Grundtvig's analysis was sound.

The German states did not remain divided. Throughout the 1800s, more and more small and medium-sized German states coalesced into one large state, in a development primarily fueled by the Prussian chancellor Otto von Bismarck. The congress formally establishing the state union took place on January 18, 1871. Italy, which had similarly not existed as a nation-state in the mid-1800s, was also united. Formally, this took place in 1861 when Vittorio Emanuele II of Sardinia joined the previously divided states of Italy into one kingdom. Following these aggregation processes in Germany and Italy, the number of states in Europe – which had once comprised several hundred principalities and monarchies – was reduced to about 21.

And what of the three small Scandinavian countries in the north: Denmark, Norway, and Sweden? Should they gather into a union? As the Danish historian Rasmus Glenthøj and the Norwegian historian Morten Nordhagen Ottesen have demonstrated in a new, comprehensive work from 2021 entitled *Union eller undergang. Kampen for et forenet Skandinavien* ("Union or demise: the battle for a united Scandinavia"), this question was extremely pressing from the 1830s to the 1860s, and a number of prominent Scandinavian politicians, diplomats, and royals strove to unite the three countries under Swedish leadership.

The idea was that a political union would ensure the survival of the Scandinavian peoples. Denmark was under pressure from the south, where Prussia's gaze was firmly fixed on the duchies of Holstein and Schleswig. Sweden was under pressure from the east, where Russia had conquered the country's eastern neighbor, Finland, in 1809. These pressures generated widespread support in Denmark and Sweden for the idea of a unified Scandinavia, which was also backed - although less strongly - in Norway. Proponents assumed that a union of states, a Scandinavian alliance, would make Scandinavia a regional power factor that would be able to withstand external pressures and promote the internal development of the three countries, as well as preventing the rivalry which had, for many centuries, been the scourge of the Scandinavian region. Prominent voices strongly advocating a Scandinavian union included the liberal Swedish parliamentarian Gustaf Lallerstedt and the Danish politician and landed estate owner Hans Rasmussen Carlsen. In fact, Carlsen was in close contact with a highly influential and outspoken Swedish supporter of a Nordic political union: the man who would be crowned Oscar II of Sweden–Norway in 1872.

In 1856, Lallerstedt published a pamphlet in French entitled *La Scandinavie*, in which he entreated: "May we, Swedes, Norwegians, and Danes (...) never fail to exploit every opportunity to safeguard our interests." He ended the pamphlet with the following appeal: "May we never forget that the goal towards which we ought to strive, and which alone can preserve our future, is the political unity of Scandinavia" (Glenthøj & Nordhagen Ottesen, 2021: 337).

Hans Carlsen was asked to join the government of Ditlev Monrad during the fateful spring of 1864. Before he did, he asked his brother-in-law, Grundtvig, whether Denmark would disappear as an independent state or have a future as a nation-state. When Grundtvig convinced him that Denmark had a future, he joined the government as Minister of the Interior. After the country's defeat in the Danish–German border war of 1864, he still put his trust in the establishment of a Nordic union. In a letter written in 1868, he concluded that "One cannot be Danish-minded without being Nordic, given that Danish is Nordic; and one cannot be Nordic without wishing, as the times and opportunities may suggest, for a closer union" (Glenthøj & Nordhagen Ottesen, 2021: 91).

Nonetheless, despite actual drafts of a Scandinavian constitution, secret negotiations, and real plans of a coup against the new Danish king, Christian IX – who came from Schleswig and was in support of the old multinational Danish state – the political unification of the Scandinavian countries never came to pass. Let us now look at what *did* come to pass, with Denmark serving as our main example.

Establishing a Danish democracy

In February 1848, yet another revolution broke out in Paris. This time the unrest spread across most of Europe, erupting in Palermo, Milan, Vienna, Budapest, Berlin, Stockholm, and Copenhagen. Here and elsewhere, citizens took to the streets, built barricades, and shouted slogans. In Berlin, during the violent street battles fought on March 18, 1848, the insurgents cried out *Wir sind das*

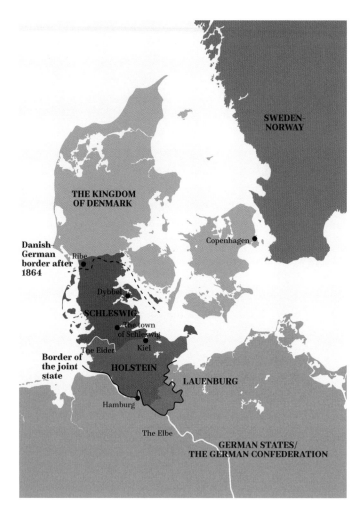

Volk ("we are the people"). Similar battles were fought throughout the European continent. Kingdoms and principalities succumbed, new nation-states were born, and new, free constitutions were written.

In Copenhagen the national-liberals – essentially a middle class consisting of the capital's *borgere*, or free citizens – organized a demonstration that walked, in a procession, through the city to address their ruler, King Frederik

VII, on March 21, 1848, demanding a people's government and a Danish state including the whole of Schleswig. That same day the king stepped down as absolute monarch, beginning the long, arduous process that would lead to the Danish Constitution, which was signed on June 5, 1849. Although the demonstration in Copenhagen on March 21 was a peaceful one, the transition to democratic rule in Denmark was not peaceful. Quite the contrary, in fact.

The emerging Danish democracy was unable to answer a crucial question: Who, and where, were the people that would rule the country? For instance, would the people living in the duchies of Schleswig and Holstein be regarded as part of a Danish people or as part of the German people, or did they constitute an independent people of their own?

The pivotal question was: Could the King's German-speaking people and his Danish-speaking people agree that they would constitute a single people – or would the new type of government also call for a new type of state? When democracy came knocking on Denmark's door in the spring of 1848, these issues were still profoundly confusing and deeply divisive. The fact of the matter was that no signed, sealed, and delivered nation-state was waiting in the wings to provide a framework for the new type of government based on the idea of the sovereignty of the people. First, the "people" who was to serve as the country's and society's supreme power had to be created. And in Denmark, as in so many other countries, this process would cost blood, sweat, and tears.

Up until March 21, 1848, the king had been the symbol of shared will and power in Denmark. However, when the king changed his position, shifting the system from an absolute to a constitutional monarchy, the result was a mutation in the symbolic order of power. Sovereignty shifted from the king to the people, making even more radical the already controversial question: Who is, and who are, the people – now that the people are no longer the King's people? Which individuals were part of the people newly destined to govern? In other words, where should the border between the Danish people and the German people be drawn? The heated debate revolved around four specific questions:

- Should the multinational, multilingual, Danish-Schleswig-Holstein joint state be upheld?
- Should Schleswig become a member of the German Confederation, as Holstein was?
- Should Schleswig become a part of the Kingdom of Denmark?
- Should Schleswig be divided?

The Danish writer and editor Meïr Goldschmidt was in favor of maintaining the multinational, multilingual state, and in favor of a border following the Elbe river. Goldschmidt emphasized Switzerland and North America as ideal examples and recommended that Denmark do the same as Switzerland, which he had visited himself and written about in detail in his journal *Nord og Syd* ("North and South"). Swiss society was not bound together by one shared language, but by a shared constitution, which moved Goldschmidt to describe the Swiss as "the only free men in Europe." In their country, he met and experienced "a new human race, with a freshness and natural candor the likes of which I have never seen before".

Back in Denmark, the national-liberals wanted to draw the border along the Eider river, which flows between Holstein and Schleswig, thereby incorporating Schleswig into the Kingdom of Denmark and separating Holstein from Schleswig. They argued that the Danish kingdom had a historical right to Schleswig, and therefore a border drawn at the Eider river was one of the main demands of the national-liberal demonstration that marched through the Danish capital on March 21, 1848 to address their king.

34

The Danish–German border issue was also discussed throughout the German states in the 1800s. In his lyrics to the anthem "Das Lied der Deutschen" ("The song of the Germans", better known by its first line: "Deutschland, Deutschland über alles", or "Germany, Germany above all"), which he wrote in 1841, the German poet Hoffmann von Fallersleben declared that Germany stretched "von der Etsch bis an den Belt" – meaning from northern Italy to the Little Belt in Denmark, which divides the Jutland peninsula from the island of Funen. Put bluntly, he regarded the then Danish duchies in the Schleswig–Holstein area as part of a united Germany. The most nationalistic Germans were prepared to swallow large chunks of the country, such as Jutland, or perhaps regard Funen and Zealand as part of an extended Sweden. In *Geschichte der deutschen Sprache* ("Story of the German language"), which the German folklorist Jacob Grimm published in 1848, the claim was even made that the belligerent Jutland peninsula was really German. Grimm declared that Jutland was a German area that was only temporarily under Danish administration, a situation that would change in the near future, given that as soon as Germany reorganized, it would be impossible for Denmark to exist as before (Adriansen 1990: 52).

It was not only the German nationalists who felt Denmark had no legitimate right to claim Schleswig. The German socialists concurred. In 1848 the socialist thinker Friedrich Engels wrote that Schleswig ought to be incorporated into Germany, and the sooner the better, as the development of history had proved that German civilization took precedence over Danish barbarism.[7]

Grundtvig explained his views on this issue in a speech he gave on March 14, 1848, presenting it as a matter of "stubborn fact" that "The land of Denmark stretches only so far as the language is spoken, and certainly no farther than people *wish* to speak Danish, in other words, somewhere that no one knows in the middle of the duchy

7. *Neue Rheinische Zeitung*, 99, quoted from *MEW*, 5, Berlin-DDR 1973, 394. I owe thanks to Per Øhrgaard for this reference

of Schleswig" (Korsgaard 2014: 116-17). Grundtvig wanted to see a country consisting of the Kingdom of Denmark, plus the part of Schleswig in which the population wished to belong to Denmark. In other words, he wanted to get the Germans out of Denmark, not through ethnic cleansing but by moving the border and making Denmark smaller – and thereby also stronger.

As discussed earlier, Grundtvig feared the sort of nationalism he saw developing in the German-speaking regions, and he considered the potential agglomeration of Germany as a major security risk and an existential threat to Denmark's survival as a state. This last fact is often forgotten today, but Danes of that day and age had to consider it carefully and prudently, which Grundtvig certainly did. In his view, it was crucial that Denmark develop a national identity that could constitute the basis of an independent Danish state. This called for the development of the rural population and an upgrading of their status, which would strengthen the core of the people.

As previously noted, the call for a democratic constitution in the Kingdom of Denmark offered no answers to the fundamental questions: Who, and where, were the people that would rule the country? Where should the border be drawn between a Danish people and a German people? Or did the Holsteiners and the Schleswegians actually constitute an independent people in their own right? The following table shows the very different and sometimes contradictory perceptions, at the time, of the region's "people" as an idea:

Table 4.1 Views on the Danish–German borderlands and their proponents

Type of state	Thinker or public figure
Dual-state solution: Schleswig/Holstein The Kingdom of Denmark	Uwe Jens Lornsen (1830)
Germany from northern Italy to the Little Belt	Hoffmann von Fallersleben (1841)
Multinational state: The Kingdom of Denmark/ Schleswig/Holstein	Meir Goldschmidt (1848)
Denmark to the Eider river: The Kingdom of Denmark and Schleswig	Orla Lehmann (1848)
Nation-state: A division of Schleswig according to the population's "Danish- or German-minded position"	Grundtvig (1848)
Schleswig merged into Germany	Friedrich Engels (1848)
Jutland merged into Germany	Jacob Grimm (1848)
A Scandinavian union	Gustaf Lallerstedt (1856) Hans Rasmussen Carlsen (1868)

Civil war in the borderlands

Soon after the demonstration in Copenhagen on March 21, 1848, a civil war broke out in the southern regions of Denmark. It lasted three years but was interspersed with periods of peace, based on truces and peace negotiations. At certain times external troops intervened, with Prussia and the German Confederation supporting the Schleswig-Holsteiners, while volunteers from Norway and Sweden supported the Kingdom of Denmark. However, both the initial encounter (fought on April 9, 1848, near Bov, a village just north of the current border) and the final great battle (fought on July 25, 1850, at Isted, near the town of Schleswig much further south) were internal clashes. In some cases brothers ended up on opposing sides.

Schleswig proved to be a problem not only for Denmark but for Europe as a whole, given that some states, such as Russia, still had absolutist rule whereas others, like England, were based on a kind of parliamentary rule. Following the inconclusive Danish Civil War of 1848-1850, the great powers of Europe, headed by Russia, issued an order in 1851 requiring that the Danish government re-create the multinational state. This involved the drafting and adoption of a "joint constitution" that would cover the entire Kingdom of Denmark, including the duchies of Schleswig and Holstein. The decision did not sit well with the national-liberal politicians in Copenhagen. They believed a joint constitution would limit the "free constitution" of 1849 and saw it as a violation of the kingdom's historical relations with Schleswig. The Holsteiners also protested, but despite very vocal opposition, in 1855 Denmark adopted a joint constitution – which, in terms of democracy, was a step backwards compared to the free constitution or "June Constitution" of 1849, as it limited the right to stand for election as one of the "people's representatives" in the Danish parliament.

Be that as it may, the joint constitution by no means brought the closure its proponents had envisaged. The Kingdom of Denmark still had a constitutional problem. The multinational Danish state continued to be weakened by the ever-stronger nationalist demands being voiced on both sides of the Danish–German "language border". The various attempts to find a solution to the constitutional problem brought the parties no closer to a solution, and the gridlocked situation drained everyone's energy and weakened the position of a state already in crisis.

In 1863, a majority in the Danish parliament tried to break the gridlock by adopting the new "November Constitution". This built on the long-standing proposal of the national-liberals, which was to draw a new Danish–German border along the Eider river. This, however, was in breach of the international agreement reached in London in 1851 after the end of the Danish Civil War. At any rate, so claimed Otto von Bismarck, Chancellor of Prussia – and by the time the geopolitical realities dawned on the Danish national-liberals, it was too late. They had been locked into an impossible position by Bismarck's tactical maneuvering and their own nationalistic agitation, and this prevented them from making the retreat that would have been necessary if they wanted to avoid another armed conflict.

For quite some time, Bismarck had been ready and willing to go to war with Denmark. He clearly expressed this in a letter he wrote in 1862: "I have no doubt that the entire Danish question can only be resolved, in a manner favorable to us, by means of a war. The reason to precipitate such a war can be found at any and every moment, as one might find most opportune for waging it" (Nielsen 1987: 33). Despite Russia's and Britain's evident interest in maintaining Denmark's integrity, Bismarck succeeded in isolating Denmark from the other great powers of Europe.

The Danes had hoped their army would be able to stop the forces of the Prussian and Austrian army at Dannevirke, an extensive but ancient earthworks fortification built across part of Schleswig. These hopes proved to be futile. When the Danish military positions near Sønderborg, defending the hills of Dybbøl, came under attack on April 18, 1864, and fell to the onslaught, Denmark's fate was sealed. The peace accord subsequently negotiated in Vienna meant that Denmark lost not only Holstein, but the whole of Schleswig as well.

The border war of 1864 marked a turning point, not only in the history of Denmark but also in the history of Germany. Having won its long-lasting territorial dispute with Denmark, under Bismarck's leadership Germany embarked on an expansionist policy that continued as it waged war on Austria in 1866, and on France in 1870-1871. These three wars dramatically altered the geopolitical landscape of the entire European continent. Denmark, with a population of two million at the time,[8] was suddenly the northern neighbor of the strongest military power in Europe – and therefore in the world. How could Denmark most prudently approach and address this new reality? The issue was fraught with tension and conflicting views. Much of the Danish population saw Germany as the enemy. At the same time Denmark's elected politicians faced the hard fact that after the 1864 war, their country now lived in the shadow of an overwhelmingly strong German empire that was chiefly consolidating its power through the use of military force.

8. As of 2021, Denmark's population was a good 5.8 million

Chapter 4.

The role of the educated middle class in nation building

In Denmark, it was mainly the middle-class citizens, most notably in Copenhagen - historically called *borgerskabet* (literally "the citizenry") - that were the driving force behind the shift from monarchy to incipient democracy. This shift from "the sovereignty of the king" to "the sovereignty of the people" happened around 1848-1849. Politically active citizens gathered into the national-liberal group mentioned earlier, which was small at first and more a network than a political party in the modern sense. This network's most prominent figures included the bishop Ditlev Monrad and the lawyer Orla Lehmann. When the first national-liberal ministers joined the government in March 1848, Monrad was appointed as the minister of culture. He regarded this newly established ministry as a "values-based ministry" that would play an immensely important role in educating "a Danish nation". Monrad envisioned creating a ministry that encompassed all the things associated with forming a national identity. In this way, even in its first faltering steps Denmark's new *folkestyre* ("people's government") emphasized that the Ministry of Culture was meant to handle everything that could promote the sort of broad formative educating it would take to create a nation.

Monrad also voiced this view in the political debate about where the administrative responsibility lay for Denmark's art museum in Copenhagen, as well as other museums. It was clear to him "that these, according to their joint interest in art and science, very nearly seem to me to belong to the undersigned ministry, which, I would venture to say, within its sphere of activity ought to comprise not only actual questions of education, but also everything that is associated with the formative education of the nation and with the mental and spiritual interests of the state in general" (Petersen 1984: 21).

Even though Monrad held *liberal* views and therefore believed in the invisible hand of the market, he also held *national* views and advocated government by means of the visible hand of the state, as well as the Danish public institutions' requirement of "propriety". Monrad considered the cultural activities of the state, in their entirety, as a fundamental element in the construction of a Danish nation. In his view, the state had the legitimacy to speak on behalf of the people, along with the associated right to intervene and regulate the people's behavior.

Monrad and several other national-liberal politicians in Denmark, who were influenced by the thinking of the German philosopher Georg W. F. Hegel, were in favor of a sort of elitist democracy. Not surprisingly, they considered themselves part of the elite that would rule the country. This thought was phrased most clearly by Orla Lehmann, the great oratorical talent of the national-liberals. In a speech he gave in 1860, he harshly criticized the parliamentary representatives of the rural classes

Ditlev Gothard Monrad (1811–1887) was a Danish bishop, politician, and cabinet minister. From 1840 to 1864 he was one of the country's most influential national-liberal politicians, and he was at the helm when the first free Danish constitution was drawn up in 1849. He is also remembered for serving as prime minister during the fateful Danish–German border war of 1864. © Wikimedia Commons

who, according to him, were abusing the general right to vote (and stand for election) to pursue special-interest politics: "When Denmark executed the dare-devil maneuver, in 1849, of transferring power to the entire people, the intention was not to place the government of the state in the hands of the uninformed peasantry." The farmers did have the right to vote, he conceded, but governing was a responsibility that fell to "the educated, the propertied, and the gifted."[9]

9. Quoted on the Danish history website www.danmarkshistorien.dk

The mainstay of the national-liberal network consisted of what was then called *dannelsesborgerskabet* ("the educated citizenry"), which was a well-informed middle class that arose in the 1800s and primarily consisted of civil servants and others in public positions of trust (pastors, lawyers, professors, lecturers, and doctors – exclu-

43

sively male). Their status lay not in aristocratic traditions or economic wealth, but rather in their level of academic and cultural erudition. After Denmark's crushing defeat in the border war of 1864, however, the national-liberals lost *political* legitimacy, while the educated middle class lost much of their *cultural* legitimacy. Both these developments were decisive to the way nationalism took shape in Denmark.

Several leading national-liberal figures doubted that Denmark even had a future as an independent nation. This was particularly true of Monrad himself, who came to personify the catastrophe, since he was the serving prime minister in 1864 when the multinational, multilingual Danish state ultimately collapsed.

During a parliamentary debate on November 5 that year, concerning a peace accord with Prussia, Monrad declared: "There is a new principal which has begun to gain ground in the ordering of European affairs (...). It is the principle of nationality, the principle of *folkelighed* [people-hood]." Seen from Monrad's position, this principle meant that it was necessary to keep fighting to the bitter end. If Denmark made peace with Prussia and relinquished the duchies of Schleswig and Holstein, it would seal the country's fate; it would merely be a matter of time before Prussia laid claim to the rest of the country. Nevertheless, rather than following Monrad's recommendation to fight to the last man, the new government chose to make peace with Prussia. In the wake of the 1864 debacle, Monrad emigrated with his family to New Zealand, tormented by a sense of loss and the fear of Denmark's demise, but he ended up returning to Denmark a few years later. Hans Carlsen tried to buy an estate in Sweden so that, at the very least, he would have somewhere in the Nordic region to go where he could be free – in the event that Denmark should cease to exist as an independent state.

State nationalism or people's nationalism

The field of political theory commonly distinguishes between political nationalism and cultural nationalism, but to describe the Danish process of nation building we also need to distinguish between "state nationalism" (a top-down phenomenon) and "people's nationalism" (a bottom-up phenomenon). The state and civil society, respectively, constitute the symbolic centers of these two types of nationalism.

As mentioned, around the mid-1800s the national-liberal movement in Denmark was strongly influenced by Hegel's ideas about state nationalism, and also by the associated notion that the will of the people ought to be managed by the educated elite. Meanwhile, the supporters of Grundtvig – called "Grundtvigians" – were inspired by Herder's ideas, mentioned above, about a "people's nationalism". Although the educated middle class in Denmark still carried some influence, after the defeat of 1864 it was the didactic objective of educating the masses, the people-as-nation, that gained a wide following and made its mark on much of Danish public life. In the power vacuum that arose after the fall of the national-liberals, the Grundtvigian proposal to educate and enlighten the people was the only movement left with any broad appeal, bearing in mind that at this point the labor movement had not yet emerged.

Unlike the national-liberal network, the Grundtvigians did not link the concept of *folk*, "people", to the state, but rather to civil society. Consequently, in a Danish context the adjective *folkelig*, "of the people or populace" (in some contexts, "popular"), became almost synonymous with "not of the state" in the traditional liberal sense.

The Danish question of the Constitution

After the loss of Schleswig and Holstein, the Danish Constitution was in need of revision. This process became a battleground for those seeking to attribute responsibility for the country's catastrophic defeat in 1864. In short: Were the national-liberals to blame? Or had the rural class let the rest of the country down, with its representatives in parliament abusing their power, as the national-liberals claimed?

These questions energized Grundtvig, spurring him to action. Never one to sit on the fence, at the age of 82 he resumed his political work and stood for election again, gaining a seat in *Landstinget*, which at that time was the first chamber or upper house of the Danish parliament (the second, "popular" chamber or lower house was called *Folketinget*, which is the name the country's unicameral parliament bears today). As the spokesman for what was then the "left wing", Grundtvig threw himself into the fray on the side of those seeking to prevent the efforts of Denmark's privileged classes to limit the election rights of the rural class, which would have given the elite a large majority in the first chamber. In Grundtvig's view, the popular vote – "general franchise" – was "so great a civil benefit that once one is legally possessed of it, one should never let go of it at any price." The new election rules would, he believed, result in "an Upper House that, at least in the people's eyes, is so far from being rooted in the general franchise that they think its real taproot is in privilege, the purse, and arithmetic, three things that at least in Denmark will never be 'of the people' [*folkelige*]."

In one of his speeches, Grundtvig came perilously close to encouraging the population, the people, to rebel, predicting that a first chamber that was *ufolkelig* (literally "*un*-popular", or "not of the people") might make the people realize – despite their wish for "everyday peace and quiet" – that at some point the better course of action may be to "fight hard for life for a while than only have the choice between a [slow, wasting] straw death and suicide."

On June 16, 1866, in the first chamber of the parliament, Grundtvig – the consummate educator and ever-controversial grey eminence of "the Danish people's enlightenment" – delivered a fierce lecture to the representatives of the upper class that they would long remember. During the parliamentary debate on the Constitution, several of them had asked: "Who are 'the people'?" To this Grundtvig replied: "It is my simple thought that inasmuch as we are all elected *by* the people, we all have the right to speak in the name *of* the people under our personal responsibility." However, the mouthpieces of the upper class found it hard to accept that *they* should speak in the name of the people, given that they did not consider themselves part of the people. Grundtvig, on the other hand, clearly understood that in a democracy one can only gain political legitimacy by referring to the people and the nation.

In the very last speech he gave in the first chamber of parliament, on July 19, 1866, Grundtvig rounded off his political career by emphasizing the two concepts that constituted the principal thread running through his political philosophy: *freedom* and *the common good*. It was his conviction that the two could not be separated without fatal consequences – which places the Grundtvigian idea of freedom outside the sphere of classic liberal thinking. Indeed, his thought is rooted in a far older republican idea, based on *res publica*, literally "the public thing", which Grundtvig rendered in Danish as *det fælles bedste* – "the common good". Thus, in Grundtvig's thinking, *freedom* and *the common good* invariably go hand in hand.

Chapter 5.
The role of the rural class in nation building

Where Denmark is concerned Grundtvig is, beyond compare, the most influential figure in the process that transformed the conception of *folket*, "the people", and brought about the Danes' sense of peoplehood. Obviously, being born in 1783 he was intimately familiar with the old meanings of the word *folk*, discussed in Chapter 2. But in 1848, in one of the numerous poems and lyrics he wrote – "Folkeligt skal alt nu være" ("'Of the people' is our watchword") – he asked his fellow Danes and communal singers[10] how one ought to understand the idea of *folk*, "people", in *this* day and age, his "now" being in the mid-nineteenth century. And what did the word *folkeligt* actually mean?

Grundtvig's own answer was deeply influenced by Herder's thoughts on language as the central component of peoplehood. But his thinking also contained an element of equality, in Danish *lighed* (literally "alike-ness"), in contrast to the class-based society which, legally and socially, was based on *ulighed* (literally "*un*-alike-ness", meaning inequality). A lover and user and coiner of words, he point-

10. The practice of communal singing, *fællessang*, is still widespread today at gatherings and, not least, in the context of *folkehøjskoler*, or "people's high schools"

49

ed to the embeddedness of the Danish word *lighed* in the word *folkelighed* ("folkish-ness" or "of-the-people-ness") if its elements are instead seen as *folke-lighed* (literally "people-equality" – tending towards the comprehensiveness of "peoplehood"). And in the first Danish constitutional assembly of 1849, Grundtvig proclaimed: "The *Age of the Estates* is over; now is the *Age of the People!*" The old ways of class-based society were at an end, ushering in the people's era.

For Grundtvig the decisive question was not the political transformation from absolute monarchy to democracy, but rather the social and perceptional transformation from the old class-based society to a new society by and for the people. In his first comprehensive history of the world, *Verdens-Krønike* ("Chronicle of the world" from 1812; he later wrote two others), Grundtvig describes a milestone decision in Denmark, taken in 1788, to abolish the institution of "adscription", a type of unfree villeinage that bound smallholders to their lord and land: "No longer can the landlords, as once they could, drag the peasant from his farm, as if dragging a horse from its stable each morning, to let him stand idle, pull a load, or trot as best they please." Now, the landlord himself must "ride his 'wooden horse' [an instrument of punishment], if he pleases, or use it for the gymnastic exercises of the young master" (Grundtvig 1905: 377).

In 1849, Grundtvig even went so far as to call the system of estates "a caste system". He was merciless in his criticism of the way the Danish class system treated the peasants, who seemed, he said, to exist like domestic animals for the sake of the other classes. Grundtvig aimed, in a sense, to turn the class-based society upside-down by lifting up the lowest caste – the rural class or "peasantry" – and making it the core of the people: "by raising the lowest of all our so-called Estates to supremacy, we are literally setting 'a peasant above his lord'." Excusing the potential distastefulness of his wording, Grundtvig maintained that it was effective to express a tendency of the times. And this tendency ought to bring gladness, since the gist of it was a movement towards freedom, equality, and *folkelighed* – "peoplehood".

This did not mean that the peasants were to become the masters of the landlords. On the contrary, they were to regard one another as brothers. The same rights and obligations would apply to farmers and landowners alike. Limitations on the personal freedom of individuals were unavoidable, Grundtvig believed, for otherwise it would be impossible to establish feasible, well-functioning societies. However, such limitations could only be justified if they were applied to all individuals and all classes:

> In my mind there is not the slightest thought of any estate's *preferential right* to enjoy freedom or leisure, nor of any person's right to shirk from whatever burdens the people must carry (...). If we are to be equally good brothers, we must equal justice enjoy; so says an old Danish proverb, and we Danes are all equally good brothers. (Grundtvig 1909: 167)

In other words, the necessary limitations would be imposed on everyone, and to the same extent.

In Grundtvig's thinking there was a decisive difference between *almuen* ("the peasantry") and *folket* ("the people"). The distinction was, above all, a matter of how a person understood the world, in terms of their self-perception and mindset. In his view, the "peasant's awareness" would have to yield, giving way to an "awareness of peoplehood". A precondition for this change in awareness and self-perception was a movement away from the collective awareness among the peasantry and into the new awareness that was characteristic of the people. What Grundtvig worked so hard to foster is what the British historian of ideas Jonathan Israel calls "a revolution of the mind" (Israel 2010: 08).

According to Grundtvig, this perceptional transformation from peasantry to people called for a new type of educational institution: a high school. Not one that offered upper-secondary education, but a *folkehøjskole* - a "people's high school" - which would accept young people studying to be public officials and civil servants (as existing secondary schools did), but which also, and notably, would accept young adults from the rural class. Grundtvig did not elaborate on or prescribe any fixed curriculum for these high schools, but he described the mandatory minimum of subjects and topics that had to be represented there: Danish, history, geography, civic studies, and, crucially, communal singing. He regarded song as an extremely important means of creating an imagined and emotional national community, with "shared public song" serving for him as a sort of social poetry that would support the norms and ideals on which the nation was being built. Grundtvig himself wrote a great number of hymns, as well as several hundred lyrical songs that dealt with the Danish people, the fatherland, and the mother tongue (Broadbridge 2015). At the people's high schools that emerged and grew across the country, gymnastics and physical exercise also took on great importance for the bodily, physical transformation of the rural class from peasantry to people.

Grundtvig's understanding of the rural population as the core of the people resonated with the efforts to promote education and peoplehood of his Nordic peers, including Henrik Wergeland of Norway, and Erik G. Geijer of Sweden. Neither of these men romanticized rustic life (nor did Grundtvig). Instead, they formulated a Nordic enlightenment project which, rather than being utopian, was pragmatically anchored in rural life and rural communities.

Henrik Arnold Wergeland (1808–1845) was one of Norway's most eminent lyricists. He also left a large and important legacy of historical works that present the farmer as the core of the Norwegian people. Moreover, he was deeply engaged in the heated political debate about language (put simply: "new" Norwegian versus "existing" Danish), and he worked tirelessly to educate and enlighten his fellow citizens. © Wikimedia Commons

In Norway, the writer Henrik Wergeland achieved cult status as a nation builder and an educator and "enlightener" of the Norwegian people. He personally published the journal *Almuen* ("The common people", 1830–1839), in which he wrote about the social problems and suppression he saw around him. On the issue of nationality, Wergeland was decidedly in opposition to one of his Norwegian contemporaries, the author Johan Sebastian Welhaven, who believed that intellectual developments in Norway ought to follow the Danish tradition. Welhaven also wanted to keep the Danish language – which was spoken in intellectual and administrative circles, particularly in the Norwegian capital of Christiania (now Oslo) – whereas Wergeland and his liberal and radical "Norwegian patriots" wanted to

Erik Gustaf Geijer (1783–1847) was a Swedish writer, psalmist, philosopher, historian, and composer. While a professor at Uppsala University he wrote *Svenska Folkets Historia* ("the Swedish people's history"), which played a decisive role in shaping Swedish self-understanding. His celebrated poem *Odalbonden* ("The farmer of Odal") from 1811 praises the role of the humble farmer throughout history. © Wikimedia Commons

do away with the influence of Danish culture and develop the country's own national identity.

The issues of language and national identity in Norway were made more complex by "the Danish era", which ended in 1814 after lasting 434 years. The question was whether the new Norwegian nation-state ought to retain its old written language, which it had shared with Denmark for several centuries, or whether it should develop its own written language. The debates over these issues grew into an intense controversy, eventually leading to the compilation and construction of a new Norwegian written language based on the country's old dialects.

A crucial difference in the nationalisms expressed in Norway and Denmark is that the Norwegian language controversy between *bokmål* ("bookish language") and *nynorsk* ("new Norwegian") was not interpreted as a conflict between two *ethnic* groups, but between two *social* groups. While "the upper class" wished to retain the old language of power (*bokmål* being quite similar to Danish), "the people" wished to speak their own "original" language. The language controversy in Denmark, on the other hand, also had to do with ethnicity, since it was interpreted not only as a social struggle between "the upper class" and "the people", but also as an ethno-cultural struggle between Danes and Germans – "the people" and "the foreigners".

In Sweden, the historian Erik Geijer wrote a hugely famous poem in 1811 about *Odalbonden*, "The farmer of Odal", characterizing those he regarded as the core of the Swedish people. Many have likened Geijer to Grundtvig, and the similarities are numerous. The two men knew each other and were kindred spirits in many ways, profoundly influencing their respective countries. Both were enormously important to the self-understanding and self-perception of their people. Both were inspired by the Romantic period and deeply fascinated by the history of their people. In addition, both regarded the earlier Enlightenment philosophers with skepticism, although both still trod the path that had been paved during the Age of Enlightenment. Finally, both contributed to developing the national consciousness of their country's rural class.

People's high schools

The first people's high school opened in Denmark, in 1844 in the small town of Rødding. This location was a logical choice: Rødding was located in Schleswig, which was still a part of the multilingual Danish kingdom at the time, although the Danish language was under pressure from Low German. The underlying reason for choosing Rødding was, therefore, the pressing question of Danish nationality. Other high schools opening around that time – between 1844 and 1864 – were founded on an interest in social issues, more specifically the poor financial situation and lack of education among the rural class, and they were not called *folkehøjskoler* ("people's high schools"), but rather *bondeskoler* ("farmers' schools") or *højere bondeskoler* ("upper farmers' schools"). One example is the high school founded in Ryslinge, a village on the island of Funen, in 1851 by Christen Kold, another prominent Danish educationalist who was deeply inspired by Grundtvig. He described his school as "an upper farmers' school" for young people aged 14 and older.

Denmark's defeat in 1864 began the heyday of the country's high schools. Over the next eight years, about 60 new peoples' high schools were founded (many of which have adapted over the years and are still actively teaching today). After Denmark lost Schleswig to Germany in 1864, the people's high school in Rødding relocated to the Danish side of the new border, moving to a small village called Askov, which lay north of the Kongeå river. Here it reopened in 1865 as Askov Folkehøjskole, and over the next hundred years the name "Askov" became synonymous with what grew into the leading high school in the Nordic region, and a powerhouse of culture and education in Denmark (Korsgaard 2019).

The project of "shaping the rural population into a people" was the motto and mission of the Danish people's high schools for more than a century. Students were expected to change their awareness and perceptions while developing vocational and scholastic skills. Virtually all the high schools combined these two aspects: giving young rural men and women a nationally formative education with a view to integrating them into a democratic community and society; and teaching them concrete skills applicable to farming and managing large households, enabling them to improve the way Danish farms were run. A classic example of this dual focus, and of the interplay between formative education and vocational schooling, is found in the first large public meeting held at brand-new Askov Folkehøjskole in 1865. The meeting consisted of three lectures on different topics: Nordic mythology; the "national question" after the loss of Schleswig; and a disorder called spavin that afflicts horses. The very same audience listened to all three lectures, learning about Nordic gods, *and* the loss of Schleswig, *and* spavin.

People's high schools were also established elsewhere in the Nordic region. In Norway, Grundtvig's thinking was mainly spread by Ole Vig, who was the son of a smallholder. Shortly before he died in 1857, at just 33 years of age, Vig gave a prophetic speech about founding a Grundtvigian people's high school in the town of Hamar. This sparked the interest of two other young Norwegians, Herman Anker and Olaus Arvesen, who traveled to Denmark and, among other things, attended the weekly lectures Grundtvig gave in the winter of 1860–1861. Because of the crisis between Denmark and Prussia, and due to the ensuing war in 1863–1864, their plans to set up a people's high school were delayed. But on November 1, 1864, Sagatun Folkehøgskole opened as the first of many people's high schools in Norway.

In Sweden, a crucial driving force in disseminating the idea of the people's high school was August Sohlman, who was an ardent supporter of Scandinavianism. Sohlman was the editor of the influential liberal Swedish daily *Aftonbladet*, and in 1867 he sent one of the newspaper's journalists on a tour of Denmark to visit a number of high schools. The coverage of the Danish high schools in *Aftonbladet* was an important source of inspiration for local politicians from the rural communities who, in 1868, initiated the establishment of the first two high schools in Sweden, one in each of the Scanian villages of Önnestad and Åkarp.

Besides the formative and educational work going on in the high schools, informative lectures, courses, and gatherings were organized by the many clubs, societies, and associations that were springing up across the region. The tradition of Nordic enlightenment was strongly influenced by liberal ideas, and being "free" - as an individual, an association, a school, or a church - meant being free both from power exerted by the state, and from power exerted by the wealthy. *Frihed* (freedom) and *frivillighed* (literally "free-willingness", or volunteerism) were seen as two aspects of the same thing. To maintain freedom it was vital that everyone was willing to do their bit as a volunteer. Associations were seen as an expression of one's communal spirit. Created and carried by the work and commitment of volunteers, they served as an ideal for the larger community of people and nation; ascertaining whether a person was prepared to voluntarily donate their time and effort, without pay, was regarded as a test of their sense of civic responsibility.

"The association", in the sense of a club or special-interest society, became the institutional backbone of the broad, popular, social mass movements that began to exert real influence on Nordic societies from around 1865 onwards. Some associations were rooted in large movements promoting a specific cause, notably including agrarian interests, women's rights, gymnastics, sports, and temperance. Others were linked to special interests, typical examples being singing, marksmanship, gymnastics, a certain people's high school or local farming community, temperance support, and, eventually, trade unions.

In Sweden and Norway the temperance movements rose to great prominence and came to exert an influence on virtually all types of associations for the better part of a century. Taking its cue from Norway and Sweden, the temperance movement also gained a foothold in Denmark. A national sobriety association called Danmarks Totalafholdsforening was founded in 1879 and mainly recruited its members in small, marginal rural communities and among urban laborers.

The Nordic countries also saw the idea of "the association" spill over into the sphere of economic activity, leading to the formation of purchasing and production cooperatives. The first Danish co-op was set up in the small town of Thisted in northwest Jutland in 1866. The initiative was taken by a cleric known simply as "Pastor Sonne", who was concerned about the poverty and difficult living conditions he saw around him, not least among urban laborers. Sonne was inspired by the workers who had united in England to fight for better conditions – twenty years earlier a group of unemployed weavers there had formed a purchasing cooperative to buy products at lower prices. Sonne's project had two aims: to give people easier access to foodstuffs, and to bring everyday democracy to "the common man". In the decades that followed, more than 2,000 co-op shops were built across Denmark.

The internationalization of the 1870s – the first step towards globalization – subjected Danish agricultural products to keen competition. Cheap grain, mainly from the United States, had found its way to the European marketplace and was there to stay. This was technically enabled by the new railway and steamship connections, allowing grain transports from the US to reach Europe at competitive prices. Even though a mounting crisis in Danish agriculture was leading to calls to impose customs on imports, the cries for protectionist policies found no political backing. Instead, the Danish agricultural community reacted to the crisis by shifting from crop-based to animal-based production. This shift called for research and new knowledge, and for reforms of the existing education of farmers, as well as a whole new processing industry of dairies and slaughterhouses, complete with a new system of distribution.

One particularly problematic question was whether this new "agroindustry" ought to be based on a capitalist model, as was the case in the emerging urban industrial production system, or on cooperative principles. Danish farmers mainly chose to organize their dairies, slaughterhouses, and distribution systems as co-ops (some of which are still operating profitably today).

The first cooperative dairy was built in the West Jutland village of Hjedding in 1882. Barely twenty years later, Denmark had 1,066 dairy co-ops across the country. The fact that farmers opted to set up these companies as cooperatives was not an obvious choice or a given decision. Every time the question of cooperative dairies was raised there was a lively debate about the business model, but the Danish dairy farmers overwhelmingly chose to organize the new refining and processing industry in cooperative companies. Many other types of co-ops also arose, processing or dealing in such commodities and services as meat livestock, fertilizer, cement, seeds, deep-freeze facilities, machinery and equipment, eggs for export, laundry, and banking services (Korsgaard 2008: 135-158).

In Denmark, Norway, and Sweden, liberal thinking was remarkably prevalent among farmers and farming communities, and this would come to play a vital role in the emergence and growth of liberal democracies in the Nordic countries.

Chapter 6.
The role of the working class in nation building

The collapse of the multinational Danish state in 1864 can be seen as an overture to the momentous changes in the state structures of Europe that took place in the wake of World War I. These changes were based on the plan that US President Woodrow Wilson presented in 1918, the year the war ended. Its main principles were that the new borders in Europe were to be drawn according to the affected peoples' right to self-determination. This concept was first expressed in the 1860s and soon spread rapidly, but only with Wilson's plan did it come to form the basis of a large and comprehensive reorganization of Europe.

Wilson's plan created the opportunity for a referendum in Schleswig on its future affiliation. In a vote in 1920, there was a majority in the northern part for a connection to Denmark, but not in the southern part. The border that was drawn and divided Schleswig in 1920 forms the border between Germany and Denmark today. However, the Danish state still consists of multiple nations, namely Denmark, the Faroe Islands, and Greenland.

Wilson's plan dissolved the two great multinational empires on the European continent – the Austro-Hungarian Empire and the Ottoman Empire – creating several new states in eastern and southeastern Europe, including Poland, Czechoslovakia, and Yugoslavia. But the result was a far cry from the emergence of new liberal democracies based on the principle of peoples' self-determination. According to the German political scientist Jan-Werner Müller, this was because from one day to the next the peasantry went from being subjects to becoming citizens: "In Central and Eastern Europe, the peasantry had become politically active for the first time, and with their mobilization appeared an explicit ideology of 'agrarianism'" (Müller 2011: 20f.). But unlike the tendency seen in the Nordics, here the mobilization of the peasantry did not become the foundation of liberal democracies.

Similarly, the British-American sociologist Michael Mann has described how difficult it was for the aristocracy and the clergy in the new states to accept the idea of peoples' right to self-determination and the principles of liberal democracy (Mann 2012). Broadly speaking, neither "the bottom" nor "the top" of such societies was able to transform itself and identify with a *demos* or people that could govern. In the interwar years the new states of Eastern Europe instead developed into autocracies that tended to lean towards fascism and Nazism.

Meanwhile, what of the working class? In 1864, Karl Marx had been the prime mover in establishing the First International, a federation of workers from different countries. The Danish chapter, set up in 1871, came to constitute the base of the Danish social-democratic movement and later political party. Its initiator was a lieutenant named Louis Pio, a self-professed anti-nationalist and advocate of internationalism. Because he regarded solidarity with workers in other countries more highly than he did the civic interests of his own nation, the Danish authorities considered him an internal enemy. The following year, in 1872, Pio was sent to prison, and later he was pressured to leave the country. The Social Democrats were formally founded as a political party in 1878 and remain an important player in Danish politics today.

For the international socialist movement, the Russian Revolution of 1917 proved to be a defining crossroads, splitting it in two: a communist faction and a social-democratic faction. Although these two ideologies had a common enemy in capitalism, they had different perceptions of democracy. Put very simply, the communists refuted liberal democracy as a way of achieving a socialist society, regarding the *dictatorship of the proletariat* as a necessary detour or way-station on their road towards a communist society. The social-democrats, on the other hand, while doubting the potential of liberal democracy, did not write off democracy as a means to achieve a socialist society.

In the years preceding the outbreak of World War I in 1914, the labor movement strongly believed in the power of the international brotherhood of workers to prevent a great war in Europe. At a meeting held in Basle in 1912, under the specter of the ongoing war in the Balkans, the prominent Danish social-democratic politician Frederik Borgbjerg declared: "The workers' international brotherhood – that is the rock upon which the church of world peace must be built. It is the grand and wonderful gospel of this day and age, and we are its preachers and the instruments of its fulfilment" (Sørensen 1943: 155). As it turned out, World War I dealt a hard blow to the workers' international brotherhood, by revealing that national solidarity took precedence over international solidarity.

Borgbjerg was the first Dane to formulate the ideological consequences that the social-democrats were forced to acknowledge in light of "the Great War". According to Borgbjerg it would no longer do to regard "the nation" as a stage in some historical development from bygone days.

Per Albin Hansson (1885-1946) was a Swedish politician who served as his country's prime minister from 1932 to 1946, with one brief intermission in 1936. Hansson is to Sweden what Stauning is to Denmark, and his legacy makes him synonymous with the epoch when the parties of the social-democrats were transformed from class-based parties into "people's parties" with a broader appeal, and from protest parties into parties with real, enduring political power. © FPG / Staff / Getty

Rather, it had to be seen as the foundation on which to realize democracy and socialism. In advocating this view he altered the traditional socialist perception of the concept of the "nation", which went from being a disparaging term to a call for unity. As Borgbjerg stated:

> We have often claimed that in our day the national idea, provided it is taken seriously, must become one with the democratic idea; the nation's freedom must become one with the people's self-government. And we have further claimed that in our day the democratic idea, provided it is taken seriously, must become one with the socialist idea – for more important than equal political influence in lawmaking is, most certainly, equal social rights relating to production

and consumption. The nation's freedom and the people's government must be extended to the very economics of society as a whole. (Bryld 1992:343)

Coupling the democratic element and the social element came to be pivotal in the perception of the "nation" that the Danish social-democrats gradually developed in the interwar years.

In Sweden, the driving force behind a similar process was Per Albin Hansson, who in his influential writings was already using the Swedish expression *folkhemmet* ("the people's home") in 1922, a term he coined to forge a link between the working class and the concept of *folket*, "the people". Hansson gave a legendary speech in 1928 in which he cemented the *folkhem* vision as a cornerstone in the very foundation of Swedish social-democratic ideology. In this vision the old notion that everyone, without exception, "belonged" as part of a household was transferred to the household of the nation-state:

The basis of the home is community and togetherness. The good home does not recognize any privileged or neglected members, nor any favorite or stepchildren. In the good home there is equality, consideration, co-operation, and helpfulness. Applied to the great people's and citizens' home this would mean the breaking down of all the social and economic barriers that now separate citizens into the privileged and the neglected, into the rulers and the dependents, into the rich and the poor, the propertied and the impoverished, the plunderers and the plundered. Swedish society is not yet the people's home. There is a formal equality, equality of political rights, but from a social perspective, the class society remains, and from an economic perspective the dictatorship of the few prevails. (Tilton 1991)

According to Per Albin Hansson, the good home constituted a model for a good society: the nation-state as a *folkhem*, a house and home where every one of the people belonged. Society ought to be transformed into a "society as community", a household that encompassed the people. This vision of the nation-state as a *folkhem* and the word itself became enormously important in Sweden, and the thinking behind the idea also gained a very large following in Norway and Denmark.

The people as race

Bear in mind that there has never been any clear, universally agreed definition or understanding of the concepts of "people/peoplehood" or "nation/nationhood". As previously noted, these words all express a notion of something shared, collective, communal. But the question of what exactly lies at the heart of this intangible "something" has been – and remains – disputed. The reason is that nations and peoples *can*, of course, be understood in a variety of ways: as communities of politics, culture, social class, language, religion, and/or race. Meanwhile, in the interwar period the question of how these words *ought* to be understood became increasingly urgent in step with the successful dissemination of the idea that an unbreakable bond existed between race and people.

This idea, the roots of which stretch far back into European history, had been gaining ground since around 1865, and it led to growing anti-Semitism across Europe. A Danish literature critic well known outside his own country, Georg Brandes, who was Jewish himself, feared the sort of nationalism he saw growing around him:

> The nationalist movement in modern Europe – whether it has an added element of religion, as in France, where it has turned against the Protestants, or whether it simply seeks its strength in racial

awareness, as in Germany – has shown itself to be anti-Semitic everywhere. It claims that men and women of Jewish descent can never achieve any deeper influence on a population that is of Romance, German, or Slavic ancestry, any more than they can be perceived as representative of such a population. (Brandes 1905: 492)

Brandes hoped that the assimilation and emancipation of Jews would "resolve" the problem, but it did not. Quite the reverse.

In *Mein Kampf*, which Adolf Hitler wrote in 1924–1925 while serving a prison sentence for a coup attempt in Munich in 1923, he claimed that the primary task of the nation-state was to ensure racial purity. In this task, Hitler believed, the "body of the German people" was in a fortunate position, as it had not been mixed as much with "the bodies of other peoples" as might have been the case. This meant that "even now we have large groups of German Nordic people within our national organization, and that their blood has not been mixed with the blood of other races. We must look upon this as our most valuable treasure for the sake of the future" (Murphy 2002). This treasure had to be protected before it was too late, and in Hitler's view it was the responsibility of the nation-state to ensure the future of the German race, "in face of which the egotistic desires of the individual count for nothing and will have to give way" (Murphy 2002).

Also in *Mein Kampf*, Hitler stressed that one is bound to a nationality "not (...) by the tie of language, but exclusively by the tie of blood" (Murphy 2002). While Herder and Grundtvig wrote about "the *spirit* of the people", Hitler wrote about the "the *body* of the people", signaling a shift away from language and over to biology as the factor that defined the people. To Hitler, people and race were essentially one and the same.

Furthermore, he did not see the Jews as parts of the people's community but as foreign elements on the body of the German nation, which, therefore, had to be eliminated. Mass relocation and genocide were the two methods Hitler employed to carry out a total "reconstruction" of Europe based on the principles of racial purity. After World War II, the Holocaust perpetrated by Hitler's regime became the ultimate symbol of the barbarism these principles had brought about.

Like other totalitarian ideologies, notably Stalinism in the Soviet Union and fascism in Italy, the teaching and education of Hitler's "national-socialism" were meant to serve the interests of the state. In *Mein Kampf*, he also presented his program for an authoritarian "educational State" with fluid boundaries between education, propaganda, and indoctrination. As he explained:

The State (...) will first of all have to base its educational work not on the mere imparting of knowledge but rather on physical training and development of healthy bodies. The cultivation of the intellectual facilities comes only in the second place. And here again it is character which has to be developed first of all, strength of will and decision. And the educational system ought to foster the spirit of readiness to accept responsibilities gladly. Formal instruction in the sciences must be considered last in importance. (Murphy 2002)

Hitler's philosophy on education bore witness to a physical, bodily turn compared to the older pedagogical approach, and training physical fitness was now declared as the school's most important task.

The ideology of Nazism forced the Danish people's high schools to take a closer look at their own ideological foundation, given that national-socialism was clearly tapping into and finding nourishment in some of the same historical-ideological and cultural roots that gave sustenance to the Grundtvigian high school tradition. For Scandinavians, many shared concepts were recognizable, albeit with the German prefix *Volk(s)*.[11] This is illustrated in some of the concepts that lie at the very heart of Nordic high school thinking, spelled here in Danish: *folk*, *folkeånd*, *folkelighed*, and *folkeoplysning*. The last of these was recognizable, for instance, in the German name of the ministry headed by Joseph Goebbels, which included the word *Volksaufklärung* ("enlightenment of the people") and is known in English as "the Reich Ministry of Public Enlightenment and Propaganda". Linguistic and connotational similarities aside, with a few exceptions the people involved in the high school movement unequivocally refuted Nazi ideology.

Flemming Lundgreen-Nielsen, a Danish scholar of Grundtvig, offers the following explanation: "All those factors that in Germany led from Herder and Fichte to the disasters under Wilhelm II and Hitler, led in Denmark to the emergence of the *people's high school*, co-operative movements and parliamentary and folk culture based on discussion and compromises – ideally always with respect for the minority" (Lundgreen-Nielsen 1992: 173).

Defining a "community of the people"

Undoubtedly, one important reason why Hitler gained such a huge following was that he promised to re-create a *Volksgemeinschaft*, a "community of the people", following the chaotic years of the Weimar Republic. However, it was only after the crash on Wall Street in October 1929 that his National Socialist Party – Nationalsozialistische Deutsche Arbeiterpartei (NSDAP) – began to gain real momentum. The collapse of the financial markets in the United States had devastating economic and social repercussions around the world. For one thing, be-

11. German was a subject taught in many Nordic schools, whose pupils would know that the German *v* in *Volk* is pronounced as an *f*, as in the Nordic variations of *folk*

tween 1929 and 1933 unemployment and poverty were widespread in the US and Europe, and particularly severe in Germany – which was a contributory factor to Adolf Hitler's rise to power in 1933. His political project was to re-create "the community of the [German] people", and the *Volksgemeinschaft* was, in fact, the official term for the societal model of the NSDAP, known for short as the "Nazis" – a word that had no explicitly negative overtones at the time, but was simply a practical contraction in the German language.

Hitler and his Nazi party were not alone in making the concept of "the community of the people" their ideological foundation. Communism and fascism were similarly eager to profess their support of the most important component of political democracy: "the people". The Italian political philosopher Giovanni Gentile even went so far as to call fascism the most valid form of democracy. In 1927 he informed the American readers of *Foreign Affairs* that "the fascist State (...) is a people's state, and as such, the democratic state par excellence" (Müller 2011: 106).

The totalitarian ideologues argued in favor of various types of welfare arrangements and systems, and Soviet communism and German national-socialism both had clear ambitions, written into their political platforms, of implementing welfare states. The German historian Götz Aly points out in his book *Hitlers Volksstaat* (2005; "The people's state of Adolf Hitler") that the Führer's welfare programs played a decisive role in the wide following he found. After assuming power in January 1933 the Nazis began to restructure the fragmented class-based society of the Weimar Republic, providing decent social and unemployment benefits and new opportunities for people to climb the social ladder. Because of this, both Soviet-style communism and German national-socialism appealed to parts of the working class in the Nordic countries.

In Denmark, Hartvig Frisch, who was the chief ideologue of the Social Democratic Party, wrote a book in 1933 entitled *Pest over Europa* ("Plague over Europe"). This made him the first to openly draw a firm boundary demarcating the line between social-democracy and communism, fascism, and Nazism. In his introduction to the book Frisch outlined the root causes of the rise of fascist regimes, making it clear that the most important task of the workers' parties was to establish a solid line of defense to protect democracy as a form of government. According to Frisch, this defense would have to consist in the transformation of labor parties into broadly founded people's parties (*folkepartier*), a development that had already begun to take place across the Nordic countries.

Frisch was particularly aware of how important it was to position the labor movement in the ideological battle that was raging. In his view, the labor movement was under pressure from communist agitation on the one hand, and fascist/Nazi-style propaganda on the other.

> Therefore, every democrat who wishes to take a position on this issue must realize that this cannot be done academically, as a theoretical choice between democracy and dictatorship, but that the current problem actually has to do with the working class's position in society and its relationship to other classes in the population. (Frisch 1933)

As the antithesis of totalitarian ideologies, Frisch put forward democracy in the Nordic region, explaining that it was the farmers who "created political democracy – that honor is theirs. It is the workers who have continued to build on this basis and poured the foundations of the *social* democracy" (Frisch 1933).

Hartvig Frisch dedicated this book to the sitting Danish prime minister, Thorvald Stauning, who is a key figure in modern Danish history. His greatest political achievement, known as the Kanslergade Agreement, was a political accord reached between the parliamentary representatives of the rural and working classes and signed on January 30, 1933 - the very same day Adolf Hitler took over as the leader of Germany.

Stauning realized his greatest *ideological* achievement in laying out a new political platform for the Social Democratic Party in 1934. It was entitled *Danmark for folket* ("Denmark for the people"), and he penned it almost single-handedly. With this ideological-political manifesto Stauning made the concept of *folket* - "the people" and by extension "peoplehood" - not just acceptable to but central in the social-democratic mindset. Adopted on May 23, 1934, the manifesto cemented the boundaries vis-à-vis non-democratic ideologies:

> We turn absolutely against attempts to rob the people of its right to co-determination. We fight against the dictatorial movement that bears the name of communism, and we fight against the various forms of fascism which have now also turned up here in Denmark. (...) The Social Democratic Party will play a part in irreconcilably combating any and every movement that threatens our community and aims to disturb the peaceful development of the arrangements and the functions of our society.

Calling his ideological-political manifesto *Danmark for folket* was a stroke of genius on Stauning's part, as he rolled the three notions of people, democracy, and state into one. He knew how dangerous it would be to leave the concept of *folk/Volk/popolo* to the totalitarian ideologies spreading across Europe. That is why it became decisive for Denmark's development in the interwar years that the country's Social Democratic Party threw itself into the in-

Thorvald Stauning (1873-1942) is exceptional not only as Denmark's first social-democratic prime minister (1924-1926) but also as the country's longest-sitting prime minister ever (1929-1942). Under the motto "Stauning or chaos," the country's Social Democratic Party once won more than 46% of the votes cast. Stauning became revered as "the nation's father". © Wikimedia Commons

tense battle being waged for the ideological ownership of the concept of "people". A multitude of voices – nationalist, communist, fascist, and Nazi – were each touting their own interpretation of it. The social-democratic voices entered the fight by defining "the people" as a national-social and democratic community – as opposed to any indigenous, biological, or race-based community.

In Denmark, the social-democrats embraced the ideas of people(hood) and nation(hood). The later Danish prime minister Hans Hedtoft emphasized in 1935 in a lecture he gave to leaders of DSU, the organization Social Democratic Youth, that the working class had to take a positive view of "the national" and "nationhood", given that the nation-state is built "on the consciousness of a shared feeling, a natural national sense of community beyond the interests of rank, estate, and class that are present within one nation or state." Throughout Danish history, the estates of the nobility, citizenry, and peasantry had all contributed to developing and sustaining the Danish nation. But now,

73

it was the workers' turn. The time had come for the labor movement and the Social Democratic Party to lead the national project onwards. This meant that politically the social-democrats had to take a new and different view of "the national". Rather than rejecting nationalist feelings as suspect, they must now be accepted. According to Hedtoft, it would simply be a blatant rejection of fact "if one were to deny the existence of the national feeling. It does actually exist as a reality, this feeling for the fatherland, and precisely over the past 20 years of European politics it has proved that it is capable of moving millions of souls among the people – including within the working class."

In Norway the workers' party, Arbeiderpartiet, under the leadership of Johan Nygaardsvold, reached a political accord with the agrarian party, Bondepartiet, in 1935, and in the late 1930s the country adopted laws instituting unemployment benefits, old-age pensions, better health insurance for all, and nine days' holiday per year. In Sweden, 1936 saw the formation of a coalition government formed by the workers' party, Socialdemokraterna, and the agrarian party, Bondeförbundet, which initiated and implemented an expansive social policy program called *folkhemspolitiken* ("the policy of the people's home") engineered by Per Albin Hansson.

In the Nordic countries, the crisis of the 1930s did not lead to national-socialism, but to the inverse and very different approach of social-nationalism. Although interlinking the principles of *socialism* and *nationalism* was a feature shared by the communism of Joseph Stalin, the Nazism of Adolf Hitler, and the socialism of Thorvald Stauning and his like-minded peers across Scandinavia, it was only in Nordic political thought that these two principles were also firmly linked to *democracy*. This is a crucial aspect in explaining why the Nordic welfare states are neither "socialist" nor indeed "communist", but instead explicitly "social-democratic".

With the Kanslergade Agreement of January 30, 1933, and similar agreements in Sweden and Norway, politicians in Scandinavia laid the cornerstones of what would later evolve into the Scandinavian model of the welfare state, based on the idea of the nation-state as the protector and "home" of the people. These broad political and parliamentary accords between representatives of the workers and the farmers – unknown outside the Nordic region – were a key component in the building of the Nordic welfare states after World War II, which were based on a combination that balances socialist and liberalist principles. In other words, these agreements were decisive elements in what has since become known as "the Nordic way".

Folkbildning – educating the people

The labor movement's contribution to *folkbildning*,[12] a Swedish concept meaning "forming and educating the people", or more loosely "popularizing education", led to a variety of educational reforms and new forms of "enlightenment" with a broader reach. Just as N. F. S. Grundtvig is referred to as "the father of the people's high school", so the Swedish socialist Oscar Olsson is celebrated as "the father of the study circle". Olsson became a leading figure in the Swedish effort to educate the wider population during the first half of the 1900s. He was inspired by the American philosopher John Dewey, whose ideas of educational and pedagogical reform he helped to introduce in Sweden, and in 1902 he organized the first-ever study group, which he called a *studiecirkel* ("study circle").

In Olsson's view, the study circle's innovations were, firstly, that it was built on people's own ability to organize and self-educate and, secondly, that books and public libraries were an integral part of its working method. Books, he explained, held the collective experiences of humankind and were accessible to everyone through libraries. Olsson's vision was that the study circle would open the door for individuals, and for the entire working class, to the universal cultural heritage of humanity, and that it would do so on each person's own terms. As workers acquired knowledge of this cultural heritage, they were to do so with a critical eye, he cautioned, as the prevailing interpretation of this culture had been formed by the upper class. Olsson hoped that the study circle format would replace that of the lecture, and the library's study hall would replace the lecture hall as the primary place of learning. Finally, study circles were meant to revolve around a shared quest for knowledge (rather than socializing), and all members were expected to take ownership and contribute.

The idea of the study circle won ground in step with the emergence and growth of the movements for workers' emancipation and temperance in the early 1900s. As a concept, a didactic method, and a practice it became an important factor in the Swedish understanding of democracy. The study circle also began to gain traction in Denmark and Norway. In Denmark a study circle society was formed in 1915, and in 1919 the social-democratic politician Harald Jensen published a small handbook entitled *Bliv Viis!* ("become wise!") on how to work in study circles. Olof Palme, who served as the prime minister of Sweden in 1969–1976 and again in 1982–1986, described Sweden, in his own signature brand of evocative phraseology, as a *studiecirkeldemokrati* ("study circle democracy"), meaning it was based on a closely woven network of study circles that spanned the entire country.

In the early decades of the push to bring education to the people, the primary target group in the Nordic region consisted of young men and women from rural areas. Then, in the early 1900s the labor movement began to establish its own high schools, aiming to educate young people from the working class. In Sweden, Brunnsvik Folkhögskola was founded in 1906 with support from the Swedish

76

labor movement. A Danish workers' high school was founded in Esbjerg in 1910 on the initiative of the editor Jens Peter Sundbo. In Sundbo's speech at the school's opening he emphasized that it had a two-fold mission: to qualify students to be a part of the country's civil democracy, and to equip them to be part of the labor movement's organizations. His inspiration was the Grundtvigian "people's high school"; in his youth he had spent three winters as a student at Askov Folkehøjskole (see Chapter 5). Even so, his view on "the national question" about Schleswig–Holstein differed from the Grundtvigian view. In fact, being an ardent supporter of internationalism, in 1912 he urged the Danish-minded workers in South Jutland to vote for the German social-democratic party rather than to cast in their lot with the Danish minority voters' association (see Chapter 3).

In 1930, the labor movement in Denmark acquired the premises of a former Grundtvigian people's high school in Roskilde, west of Copenhagen, and transformed it into a workers' high school. The intensely symbolic inauguration took place on a national holiday, Whit Monday 1930, and the keynote speaker was the country's leading social-democrat and prime minister, Thorvald Stauning. His speech emphasized that the working class had historically been ridiculed as ignorant – lacking knowledge, refinement, and culture – a situation that would have persisted had the workers not created their own educational network.

His keynote was followed by a speech from the new school's headmaster, who explained that Grundtvig's thoughts on "popular enlightenment" (folkeoplysning) and democracy had provided the impetus for the first high schools. Now the time had come for the workers' high schools to "serve a new phase in the democratic development." The headmaster found Grundtvig's phenomenal powers of prediction to be verified in the way he went

77

against the individualism inherent in liberalism by stressing "that a human life only reaches its full accomplishment when shared with others in community." Quite naturally for Grundtvig, the types of sharing and community he was referring to were of a national and religious nature, the headmaster noted, and now it was just as natural to refer to communities that were social and international.

The last speaker was Frederik Borgbjerg, the social-democratic minister of education, who sincerely hoped that all the best in Grundtvig's thought would live on at the workers' high school. The ceremony ended, as was customary, with communal singing – although the choice was not one of Grundtvig's many traditional high school songs, but the socialist movement's "Internationale".

As discussed earlier, the social-democrats in Denmark rallied behind the idea of a "community of the people" but at the same time distanced themselves from the concept of "people" as used by the totalitarian ideologies. Borgbjerg, for one, made this stance explicit, for instance by referring to the difference between the way Hitler and Grundtvig understood "the people". In 1933, on the 150th anniversary of Grundtvig's birth, Borgbjerg gave a speech, printed in the newspaper *Social-Demokraten*, that held up Grundtvig as a bulwark against the anti-democratic currents of the times: "He was a true son of the century of enlightenment and 'an apprentice of the Germans' (...), but not a supporter of Bismarck's and Hitler's Germany. (...) The Danish people's resilience against the contagion of Nazism and Fascism is due, not least, to Grundtvig's enormous effort to educate the people". That year, in the daily *Politiken*, Borgbjerg also referred to how Grundtvig had become "a zealous supporter of the free people's government and the most extensive degree of free suffrage" – like a genuine democrat.

Chapter 7.

The demos strategy

World War II intensified the importance attributed to "people" as an idea, and also sparked discussions about it as a concept. Denmark and Norway were occupied by German forces on April 9, 1940. After a few military engagements the Danish government decided to capitulate, subsequently declaring that it would continue to govern, albeit under official protest. Soon afterwards, a "national unified government" was formed, which went on to govern Denmark until August 29, 1943, acting at times as instructed by the occupation forces, and at times against their instructions. Following the breakdown of negotiation politics, the Nazis stepped in and installed a "general government" of Denmark, which lasted until the German capitulation was announced on May 5, 1945.

After the country's occupation in 1940 the consensus was that the situation called for "national unity", but this phrase meant very different things to different individuals and parties. During the first few months of occupation two main understandings of "national unity" took shape.

One was that the nation had to be elevated again by toning down democracy: dissolving the parliamentary system, getting the government to step down, and instead appointing a government consisting of "the best men of the realm". Western European democracy had played out its role as a political system and could not be resuscitated, the argument ran. Views of this sort came not only from actual dictator states but also from figures in democratic countries like Denmark. An example is the prominent but controversial writer and pastor Kaj Munk, who was no admirer of democracy but who, until the German occupation of Denmark, was deeply fascinated by forceful political leaders like Mussolini and Hitler.

The other understanding was that achieving "national unity" in support of Danish democracy was the best way forward. Rather than any military defense of the *state*, this was a rallying call for a cultural defense of the *nation* – in short, a project of nation building. What would be put to the test in this understanding was whether the integrity of the cultural or mental nation of Denmark could be maintained even though the territory of the physical state of Denmark was occupied.

The German occupation further cemented Grundtvig's position as a figure that could unite the nation. On September 18, 1940, at the University of Copenhagen, a professor of church history named Hal Koch delivered the first in a series of lectures he would give about Grundtvig. An audience of more than 500 crowded into the lecture hall, many of them forced to stand; consequently he gave each of his following lectures twice, at separate times.

This lecture series was one of the reasons why, in the autumn of 1940, Koch was chosen as the chairman of Dansk Ungdomssamvirke (DU; now DUF, the Danish Youth Council), an umbrella organization meant to prevent the Nazification of Danish adolescents and young adults. Immediately after the occupation steps had been taken to protect the country's public institutions against Nazi infiltration, an issue of crucial concern in all occupied countries. Koch's ambition in his work with DU was to politically energize the Danish youth community in favor of democracy:

> It has been strongly emphasized that DU is apolitical. To my mind this is a dangerous statement. If DU contributes to de-politicizing our young people at the same time as national sentiments are being reinforced and the value of sport is being stimulated, then the Danish Youth Council will be directly contributing to the Nazification of Denmark's young generation. (Nissen & Poulsen 1963: 136)

Many people were surprised by Koch's understanding of "nationality" in the sense of "What makes a nation?" Going against the prevailing conception of Danishness, he rebuffed the idea that what bound Danes together was a shared culture and language. As he put it: "What is shared, the commonality, is finding another place. What fundamentally binds us together is the *political* sphere," by which he meant democracy (Koch 1942: 17).

In Hal Koch's view, the war was not primarily among or between nations, but between two political systems: democracy and totalitarianism. In the battle against the occupying forces the object was therefore to strengthen and maintain a democratic mindset in Denmark, especially among young Danes. Unlike the Nazis, who extolled national values, he urged the Danes to guard and uphold democratic values. The acid test of Danishness, in Koch's view, was whether the Danish Jews were regarded as fellow Danes and compatriots. After the occupation began, the ever-pressing question was what consequences the occupying power's anti-Semitic ideology would have for Denmark. When, in late 1941, rumors began to circulate

Hal Koch (1904–1963) was a Danish professor of church history. During the German occupation (1940–1945) he was the chairman of the Danish Youth Council, which was established to prevent the "Nazification" of the country's adolescents and young adults. After the war, in 1946 Koch founded Krogerup Højskole, a people's high school that focused on democracy and civic engagement. © Scanpix Danmark/Nf-Nf/ Ritzau Scanpix

about the imminent deportation of the country's Jews, Koch forged an unbreakable bond between the fate of the Danish nation and the fate of the Danish Jews. As he put it, to doubt their status as fellow citizens was tantamount to throwing away the most precious element embodied in the entire concept of Danishness.

As long as the still-Danish government's politics of negotiation continued to work the Danish Jews were safe, since the government's political agreement with the occupying power relied on the precondition that Danish Jews were not to be sent to the German concentration camps. But when this politics of cooperation broke down on August

29, 1943, the Jews were no longer under the protection of the Danish government – which had ceased to exist. As the Germans planned the deportation of Denmark's Jewish population, scheduled to begin in October that year, a large-scale civilian rescue operation was set in motion. With the assistance of numerous Danes and Swedes crossing the waters between the two countries, almost all of the Jews in Denmark were transported to safety in Sweden, a neutral country in the war, thereby avoiding Hitler's concentration camps. In total, more than 7,000 Jewish Danes were rescued in this operation, which places it among the largest distinct initiatives to counteract the Nazi persecution of Jews during World War II.

Expanding the concept of democracy

A new approach that would become known as "the demos strategy" was being developed during World War II. The gist was to convince ordinary people that democracy was worth fighting for. However, this could not be done merely by referring to the concept of democracy in terms of its formalities, international legal framework, or methods of representation, so it became necessary to expand the concept of democracy to other areas beyond the political sphere.

Throughout the history of democracy, there have always been critical voices speaking out against the formalized concept of democracy based on the laws of the state. However, it was only with World War II that this critique gained any major following. The demos strategy called for an expansion of the concept of democracy, bringing it to new areas of public life. In general, progressive efforts were made across Europe during and after the war to fulfill this requirement to expand democracy to the economic, social, educational, and cultural spheres.

In Sweden the couple Gunnar and Alva Myrdal, who were both prominent social-democrats, were strong advocates of the demos strategy. In her book *Nation and Family* from 1940, published in Swedish in 1944, Alva Myrdal stressed that the end of World War II would bring about a call for *social* democracy across Europe. According to her:

> The Scandinavian countries, and particularly Sweden, have by an historical accident been given a most advantageous set of prerequisites for a bold experiment in social democracy. Consequently, these countries will have to give an account as to whether they have envisioned a democracy that really works for its citizens. (Myrdal 1940: 10f.)

In Denmark, Hal Koch became a leading advocate of the demos strategy. By virtue of his position as the chairman of the Danish Youth Council he demanded that the demos strategy be made an integral part of the country's official policy after the war. In his view, one of the main reasons for the rise of national-socialism was the economic and social crisis of the 1930s. It was therefore essential, he said, to democratize the country's economic and social activities; he considered democracy as a *form of government* to be dependent upon both democracy as a *way of life* and democracy as a *model of society.*

Koch regarded democracy as more than formal procedures, encompassing social aspects – solidarity with the most vulnerable members of society. "I do not believe in any long-lasting political democracy without it having, as its foundation, a continuously progressing realization of economic democracy. It is no use to become so intellectual that one denies the fact that it is first and foremost the economic conditions that determine what a society is like" (Koch 1966: 39).

These views were clearly expressed in Denmark in the political platform adopted by the Social Democratic Party in 1945. Entitled *Fremtidens Danmark* ("Denmark in the future"), this platform emphasized that "the democracies must demonstrate not only that they can win wars, but also that they can create social security."

After the war, the social-democratic parties became the motivating force behind ongoing efforts to give the democratic state a social form or manifestation. Central to this type of state was the idea that the public authorities would actively work towards creating symmetry between the state's inhabitants by compensating for the asymmetries created by the market.

This goal led to major political disputes between supporters of the two types of state: a liberal, law-based state on the one hand, and a social-democratic regulatory and redistributing state on the other. The battle was clearly won by those who supported the latter.

As for the size and scope of the state, there is a remarkable difference between the two types of states. The option embodied in the former is a very limited range of authority, whereas the latter can allow expansive state regulation, the scope of which is decided by what is necessary to realize the goals of the politicians. If the liberal state is seen as passively anticipatory, then the social-democratic state must be seen as actively regulatory. The welfare state was meant to compensate for the inequalities of the market, redistributing wealth among classes and groups in the population. In concert with the building of welfare states in Denmark, Norway, and Sweden, the range of socio-economic rights grew – to such an extent that gradually these rights came to receive more attention than the classic civil rights and civil liberties.

The backdrop for the population's increased trust in the state as a regulating factor was, without doubt, the crisis and mass unemployment of the interwar period. After 1945 there was greater acceptance of the view that public intervention in the workings of the market economy were meant to insure society against similar problems and, at the same time, facilitate social progress. The economy had to be subjected to political regulation, striking a balance through the creation of social security programs and increased equality, which were seen as a precondition for continued economic growth.

Chapter 8.
The welfare state as nation building

Nowadays the welfare state is often regarded as a bureaucratic machine installed to ensure a certain level of redistribution of the resources available in a given country. This, however, is a very one-dimensional view. Since its inception the welfare state has been an important part of creating and maintaining a country's national identity. In other words, there is an intimate link between nation building and the rise of the welfare state – which is found in a wide variety of different forms around the world. The extensive "Nordic welfare model" is just one of many types, as described in the well-known book *The Three Worlds of Welfare State Capitalism* (1990) by the Danish sociologist Gösta Esping-Andersen.

Once again using Denmark to exemplify, the Danish welfare state has roots that stretch back to the late 1800s. A generation of politicians marked by the country's shattering defeat to Germany in the border war of 1864 enacted and implemented the first groundbreaking laws on social reform in 1891–1892: a revised "poor law", a tax-financed allowance for the elderly, and a law on voluntary health insurance.

The next great step was taken in 1933 by the social-democratic minister of justice, Karl Kristian Steincke, following the above-mentioned Kanslergade Agreement. His pioneering socio-political work was to move financial aid to the disadvantaged out of the private sphere, ensuring all Danish citizens equal social rights and so removing the distinction between "worthy aid recipients" and those deemed "unworthy" of charity. According to Steincke, social legislation in Denmark ought to express "the regulatory, supervisory, and curative activities of the state" (Christiansen 2007). Nevertheless, what came to be called "the welfare state" did not really begin to take shape until after World War II.

The first time the phrase "welfare state" was used in a Danish context was in the book *Mennesket i centrum - bidrag til en aktiv kulturpolitik* ("The human being at the center - contributions to an active cultural policy"), published in 1953 by a group of young social-democrats. Since that time the welfare state has become the central topic of virtually all political debate conducted in Denmark.

The Danish and, more broadly, the Nordic welfare model as developed after World War II is financed by taxes. The basic principles of this model mean firstly that all those living in the country have access to social benefits, regardless of their social background or origins, and secondly that these benefits are not associated with any insurance contribution or any other type of user fee. Regarded as an ideal type, the Danish model is also called "a universal welfare model" because everyone has the right to a variety of benefits - from an old-age pension to a child allowance - that are not granted based on a needs assessment.

By way of example, a law was passed in 1956 that entitled all Danish citizens to a basic old-age pension, regardless of their income. According to a feature article published in *Socialdemokraten* on October 23 that year, Jens Otto Krag - who at the time was the minister of economic affairs and labor, and later became prime minister - believed this was very important for people's "feeling of being a member of society with rights. Democratic freedom has been provided with social content". The political goal was to introduce social rights that would give all individuals equal status in the eyes of the state and make them independent of the market.

The welfare state was built in parallel with the large demographic and socio-economic shifts that began in the 1950s and have essentially continued up to the present. In Denmark, the Social Democratic Party was its main architect and led the first efforts after the war. Since then, however, virtually all major social reforms in the country have been adopted and implemented with the support of the four "old parties": the social-democrats (abbreviated as "S"), which grew out of the labor movement; the liberals ("V"), which had their roots in the peasant movement; the social-liberals ("B"), established in 1905 after they broke away from the liberal party; and the conservatives ("K"), whose historical base was the urban bourgeoisie.

As the Danish historian Niels Finn Christiansen has emphasized, "This consensus has given Danish welfare legislation a robustness that stretches beyond the changing majorities at the elections, and it is characteristic that the right-leaning governments of 1968-1971 and 1982-1993, not to mention the 'K+V' coalition government of 2001, did not contest the basic elements of the welfare systems" (Christiansen 2007: 16). Today, the welfare state lies at the heart of what it means to be a Dane:

> The Danish welfare state is now in our blood. It is red and white, like our corpuscles and like the Dannebrog [the Danish flag]. And woe unto anyone

89

who dares to insinuate that it may not be as unique-
ly Danish as we think; or worse still, woe unto anyone who wishes to radically change it, and let us not
even mention anyone wishing to disband it. What
does it matter that it shares lots of features with the
other Nordic welfare states, and perhaps with similar arrangements in distant lands? No, the Danish
welfare state is Danish in a particularly Danish sort
of way. Politicians and voices in the public debate
daily confirm us in this belief. To think otherwise is
un-Danish. (Christiansen 2007: 25)

In similar fashion, the Norwegian and Swedish welfare states lie at the heart of what it means today to be,
respectively, a Norwegian or a Swede.

Schooled into democracy and human rights

The standard-bearers of the welfare state in the
Nordic countries considered school reform an absolutely
decisive precondition for the development of the welfare
state and of democracy. Among those who held the flag
highest were the Swedish couple Alva and Gunnar Myrdal, who worked together and published a book entitled
Kontakt med Amerika ("Contact with America"), which appeared in Danish in 1946. Based on their two study trips
to the United States in 1929-1930 and again in 1939-1940,
their book described American society, particularly the
American school and educational system. The US, they
wrote, was like a "laboratory of pedagogical progress", referring repeatedly and with enthusiasm to the pedagogical philosophy of the educationalist John Dewey and the
belief among American progressivists that society could
be steered in a more democratic direction by public,
child-centered, democracy-oriented schooling and education (Myrdal & Myrdal 1946: 91-92). The Myrdals emphasized the basic values clearly communicated in American

schools: "They serve to uphold democracy and the ideals of freedom, which is reflected in both the social structure of the schools – meaning in the way the teaching itself was organized – and in the content of the lessons and the arrangement of the personal instruction." That is why education and schooling were such an important public matter in the United States, as opposed to virtually all other spheres of American activity, where individualism and private initiative were esteemed more highly than social responsibility.

Even so, the Myrdals pointed to the unresolved dispute among American educationalists between a "liberal humanism" and a "democratic humanism", which corresponded to the tension between giving children an individualistic upbringing so they would do well in "the competitive society", and giving them a democratic upbringing so they would do well in "the collaborative society" – with Dewey and his similarly minded peers in the latter camp. "It is this choice that American education has not yet made." The Myrdals therefore encouraged "social-democratic Scandinavia" to very consciously make this choice, for if "democracy is to win over individualism, collaboration over competition, this ought to be stipulated as a goal" (Myrdal & Myrdal 1946: 96).

The educational reforms in the Nordic countries were meant to enable schools to carry out two main tasks. One was to create economic growth, and the other was to foster greater equality in society. These two tasks were linked together by the notion that economic growth and social alignment were mutually conditional. Generally speaking, although school and educational policy were seen in the light of potential economic growth, the school itself ought not to be organized based on this perspective. The task of the school was to create equality and, in so doing, contribute to economic growth.

To create greater equality in society, the school was supposed to be free of the sort of competition that governs economic activities. In popular terms, it was meant to be a "competition-free" institution. A delimitation had to be made between schools, on the one hand, and capital interests, the market, and production on the other. The "unified school" was developed under the protection of this ideological delimitation, its primary task being to give children the opportunity to develop into free, independent, democratic members of society. As such the school was to focus not only on the acquisition of knowledge and skills, but also on teaching democracy and promoting human development.

One might think that in Denmark democracy became a central pedagogical principle soon after it was introduced as a form of government in 1849, but this was emphatically not the case. For almost a century, "democracy" was not even raised as a concept in the educational system. This did not mean that educators did not value or support democracy, but it did mean that Danes regarded strong national-cultural values as a necessary precondition for having a democratic government. Education and instruction were built on a model in which democracy was a sort of add-on: The fundamental framework consisted of the people's language and culture – and, to a degree, their religion – overlaid with democratic government. Without a solid foundation there could be no democracy, which is why the school's primary task was to build a strong foundation. One way to do this was to teach Danish literature and Danish history as core subjects in the formative education pupils received. Hal Koch, in contrast, emphasized that rather than being based on a *way of life that cultivated national culture*, the foundation of democratic government was based on a *way of life that fostered democratic culture.*

In his book *Hvad er demokrati?* ("What is democracy?") from 1945, Koch argued – as John Dewey had done in *Democracy and Education* from 1916 – that democracy is not only a way of governing, but also a way of life, as noted earlier. Therefore the pedagogical approach ought to promote democratization of the individual, for "although one might succeed in carrying out political and economic democratization of a society, little will have been achieved if one does not accomplish the democratization of people – shaping, educating, and informing them" (Koch 1945).

The war had shown how important it was that the pedagogical approach became democratic. To avoid backsliding into totalitarian ideologies, education was the means of pulling individuals and society as a whole in a democratic direction. As the prominent Danish architect and cultural critic Poul Henningsen commented in an article in 1945: "Pedagogical democracy is and will remain the first weapon we ought to mobilize in defense against the danger of Nazism. It has the advantage of expanding and promoting democracy instead of restricting it."

All the experience gained from dealing with Nazism and pervasive racism across Europe in the interwar years had deeply marked both the pedagogical debate and the use of concepts related to nationhood, democracy, and peoplehood. After the war, the word "national" took on a negative ring, whereas "democracy" was perceived as extremely positive. The concepts of "people" and "peoplehood" (*Volk* in German) came to hold extremely negative connotations in Germany, whereas they retained their positive overtones in the Nordic region. Even so, the language of celebratory speeches and rallies shifted, as the use of *folk* waned while *demokrati* gained ground.

As mentioned earlier, before World War II the idea was widespread that there are fundamental differences between people. Various types of race theories set out guidelines for what could even be said about the origins of humankind and the appearance and value of human beings. This rubbed off on related academic disciplines such as history and geography, and also affected the way these subjects were taught at primary and secondary schools. Only after the immensity of the Nazi regime's persecution of the Jews became known did the wider world realize the necessity of doing away with the notion of discrimination inherent in racism, and instead promoting the notion of equality embodied in humanism. The consensus was that such an effort would require massive information campaigns provided mainly through the educational system, from primary and secondary schools right up through universities.

Even before the war had ended, the Allies had been working to create a stronger international body than the League of Nations. The final negotiations took place in San Francisco in the spring of 1945, and on June 26 that year 50 countries signed the Charter of the United Nations – the

UN. In November 1945, this body formed the organization UNESCO, an acronym reflecting its purpose of promoting international cooperation on education, science, and culture, as well as respect for human rights and democracy.

UNESCO was the driving force behind the largest and most widely coordinated post-war effort to challenge and refute the biologically grounded view of humanity, becoming a central actor in the efforts to develop a new view of humanity. The organization was supported by an extensive media apparatus, and its campaign was so enormous that about half of the works appearing in the field of anthropology in the early 1950s were published by UNESCO and written by scholars and scientists – sociologists, anthropologists, and geneticists – who were critical of race theory and were carefully and purposefully chosen (Duedahl 2007).

International understanding and cooperation became central elements in the ongoing endeavor to break down the perception of "people" as a race-based concept. In Denmark, the adjective often used to describe such initiatives was, and still is, *mellemfolkelig* (literally "inter-people", or "people-to-people"). In 1954 the Danish ministry of education authorized a number of selected primary and secondary schools to test changes to the curriculum that would promote international "people-to-people" understanding. Then, enacting a new law for the Danish *folkeskole*, the public system of comprehensive schools, in 1958 the country officially adopted UNESCO's policy for education and textbooks. A ministerial report from 1960, which set out educational guidelines and detailed the purpose of the new law on comprehensive schools, emphasized that children were to learn about people-to-people understanding and tolerance. Describing the purpose of school instruction in history and social sciences, the report stressed how important it is:

that children become accustomed to regarding problems from the viewpoint of equal rights among all peoples (....). The UN and its particular organizations must be incorporated into the instruction given by seeking to depict the work they perform in a way that is concrete and realistic, keeping in mind the aim of making the children interested in the ongoing efforts to solve the shared problems of humanity through beneficial, peaceable international cooperation. (Duedahl 2007: 252)

The landmark rejection of the biologically founded view of humanity came in 1965, when the UN adopted its International Convention on the Elimination of All Forms of Racial Discrimination. In the international community, this convention was the first binding document to denounce discrimination based on a person's biological heritage. Not only did it make discrimination politically incorrect; it also made it illegal, as the principles gradually became incorporated into the national legislation of the UN's member states (Duedahl 2007).

Once again using Danish history as a case in point, a new School Act adopted in 1975 saw the word *demokrati* written into an article that sets out the very purpose of its school system, for the first time in the country's history: "The public comprehensive school shall prepare its pupils for living, contributing, and co-determining in a democratic society, and for taking co-responsibility in solving shared tasks. The school's teaching and daily work in its entirety must therefore build upon freedom of thought and democracy."

Chapter 9.
Who is
– and who are –
the people?

Up until the 1960s the Nordic countries were fairly homogeneous in terms of ethnicity, culture, and religion. They have since become more diverse, and gradually certain questions have grown ever more pressing: Who is considered part of "the people"? And what does "national identity" mean today? These questions mainly arise in connection with three overlapping discussions that concern Europeanization, migration, and the welfare state.

Europeanization

Around 1970, the themes of peoplehood and national identity re-emerged as a central and contentious issue in Denmark and Norway. This was occasioned by the referendums held in 1972, one in either country, to determine whether they would join the European Communities (EC; now the European Union, EU). In the third Scandinavian country, Sweden, which did not apply for EC membership at the time, the issue of national identity did not arise in earnest until the early twenty-first century brought an up-surge in migration.

The date October 2, 1972, is a milestone in Danish history.[13] This was the day a majority of the Danish popula-tion voted to have the country join the EC, thereby surren-dering or officially "delegating" sovereignty as defined in Section 20 of the Constitutional Act of Denmark "to such an extent as shall be provided by statute." This effectively meant farewell to the country that had been built on the foundation of democracy and nation-statehood established around the mid-1800s. The EU is not merely an interna-tional organization, similar to the United Nations (UN) or the North Atlantic Treaty Organization (NATO); its legal framework – and the competence of the European Court of Justice (ECJ) – carries the same legal weight in national legal systems as the member states' own legal frameworks enacted by their national parliamentary bodies. The del-egation of sovereignty in 1972 therefore lay in Denmark's commitment to follow a number of agreements and deci-sions made at a supranational level.

Around that time, many of those engaged in the people's high school movement also became active and fervent opponents of Danish EC membership, and joined an anti-EC organization called Folkebevægelsen mod EF ("The people's movement against the EC"). It is easy to follow their reasoning, since their schools had been par-ticularly important in the Danish efforts to propagate the idea of *folket*, "the people", as the ideological foundation of the state. As the Danish literary critic Jørgen Bukdahl wrote in 1961, the people's high schools were the primary driving force behind "infusing content into the concept of a Danish nation-state".

The editor of *Højskolebladet*, the periodical of the people's high school movement, commented in 1972 on the outcome of the referendum in an editorial that un-doubtedly reflected the general attitude in the movement:

13. Denmark, Nor-way, and Sweden have each held an independent referendum on whether to join the EC/EU. On 24-25 September 1972 the Norwegians voted "no"; on 2 October 1972 the Danes vot-ed "yes"; and on 13 November 1994 the Swedes voted "yes". Although Norway is not a member of the EU, the country maintains close ties with it, and espe-cially with its single market

For a publication such as (ours), the result of the referendum held on 2 October must naturally be a disappointment. To say otherwise would be dishonest. A disappointment because the views of a people's government and an identity of peoplehood which we, and many others, have laid out has been rejected by the majority of the Danish people.

A battle had been lost, but a new battle could be won, someday, somewhere down the line. "The large group of opponents may be a ray of light in the dreary Denmark we will be inhabiting after October 2."

Despite this initial attitude, after the fall of the Berlin Wall on November 9, 1989, and all that followed in its wake, in the 1990s it became harder to find people in the high school movement who disapproved of EU membership. Overall, anti-German sentiments in Denmark evaporated almost miraculously overnight. Germany is now considered one of the most stable and smooth-running democracies in Europe, and a dedicated advocate of strong pan-European cooperation within the EU. This development resembles what happened long before in Denmark's relationship with its erstwhile arch-enemy, Sweden: a gradual transition from mutual antagonism into friendship.

The European integration process gained new momentum after Russia's attack on Ukraine on February 24, 2022. Even before the invasion the question of European sovereignty had been raised as an urgent issue. Jean-Claude Junker, the president of the European Commission from 2014 to 2019, argued that Europe had to assert its sovereignty and take its fate into its own hands. The French president, Emmanuel Macron, agreed and is currently working to promote what he calls the "strategic autonomy" of Europe.

European sovereignty would require the populations of the European countries to develop an idea of belonging to a "European people". But what would that mean? Would "people" in this context be understood as a political, cultural, or social category? The German political philosopher Jürgen Habermas strongly recommends distinguishing between a political and a cultural level. Culturally, one should not seek to create a single European people; but politically, one should. The community of justice, he advises, should be raised up to a supranational level. In other words, the aim should be to create not a European *ethnos*, but rather a European *demos*, which can handle and safeguard the common interests peoples and states have in ensuring political, economic, and social stability in Europe – stability that the nation-states can no longer ensure on their own (Elias & Habermas 1994).

In Habermas's view, the process of abstraction involved in establishing the European "we" is not fundamentally different from the one that created the sense of "we" arising in the nation-states during the nineteenth century. The latter was the result of an abstraction away from dynastic communities towards national and democratic communities. So why, Habermas asks, should it not be possible for such a collective process of learning and education (in German: *Bildung*) to continue?

The weak link in Habermas's analysis is the issue of identity. As mentioned, he has no intention of linking cultural identity and political rights, yet the risk of distinguishing too sharply between culture and politics is that the entire project comes to lack the power – the energy – that lies in fusing the two elements. How to handle this issue seems to be one of the key challenges facing the greater project of the EU.

Many would claim that "a European people" would have to exist before it would be possible to establish a European *demos*. But as we learned earlier, there was no "Danish people" waiting in the wings to establish Danish democracy in 1848. There was a concept of "people", *folk*, before the country installed democracy, namely in the form of an old understanding of "people as household members". But the new understanding of "people as *demos*" was only gradually created through a dramatic process of inclusion and exclusion. In other words, a *demos* was created by imbuing the concept of "people" with new meaning, in Denmark and in many other nation-states.

In many ways, Europe currently faces the same challenge the Danish monarchy faced in 1848, at a time when the crucial question was: Was it possible to establish a free constitution in the existing multinational and multilingual state? At that time it was not possible to establish a *demos* in the state consisting of Holstein, Schleswig, and the Kingdom of Denmark. Whether it might be possible today, some 175 years later, to create a European *demos* that can make up the core of a multinational union remains an open question. Much depends on our understanding of the concepts underlying such a union. If, by "people", we understand the European *ethnos*, then surely such a construction is neither possible nor desirable. If, on the other hand, we understand "people" as *demos* – in other words, if we maintain a political understanding of the concept – such a construction is not impossible to imagine.

Migration

Migration is not a new phenomenon in the Nordic countries. From the mid-1800s to 1930 a mass emigration actually took place out of the Nordic region. During this period about 320,000 Danes and 754,000 Norwegians moved to the United States. A total of 1.3 million Swedes left their country, with 1 million traveling to the US. Many of these people were what, in modern terms, we would call economic refugees. For centuries people were migrating from Europe to America, whereas the current trends show people migrating towards Europe.

Migration – *emigration* and *immigration* – seems to be a ubiquitous element in globalization processes. Over the past 50 years, Western European nation-states have had to accommodate a rising number of people and groups from former colonies and non-European cultures. This has led to greater ethnic, religious, and cultural diversity in most European nation-states, to an extent never before seen in modern history.

What consequences does migration have for the concept of "people" and for national identity? These questions have become central themes in current debates across the Nordic region. Which individuals or groups belong to "the people", and what does "belonging" to a people mean? Does it imply being a part not only of a national *demos*, but also of a national *ethnos*?

Migration has also led to a discussion about the relationship between national identity, trust, and the Nordic welfare model. This model builds on "us", in our capacity as residents and/or citizens, being willing to pay high taxes that finance social benefits paid to people we do not know. We are therefore obliged to believe in the system, for instance trusting that those who receive the benefits actually need the money.

There are various theories about how migration affects or will affect the Nordic welfare states. Although the conclusions are far from unambiguous, there seems to be a clear-cut correlation between a Nordic/Scandinavian national identity, high levels of trust, and comprehensive public welfare arrangements. This is a point that Francis Fukuyama emphasized in his book *Trust: The Social Virtues and the Creation of Prosperity* from 1996, which he reiterates in *Identity*, published in 2018:

If members of a society feel that they are members of an extended family and have high levels of trust in one another, they are much more likely to support social programs that aid their weaker fellows. The strong welfare states of Scandinavia are underpinned by their equally strong sense of national identity. (Fukuyama 2018: 130)

According to Fukuyama, maintaining a strong national identity requires two things: firstly, that new arrivals to the country take on the role of "fellow inhabitants" and identify with the country's political culture; and secondly, that the understanding of the national identity is based on the country's existing diversity. "The challenge facing contemporary liberal democracies in the face of immigration and growing diversity is (...) to define an inclusive national identity that fits the society's diverse reality, and to assimilate newcomers to that identity" (Fukuyama 2018: 142f.).

Fukuyama regards "nations" as political units, and "assimilation" as identifying with a country's political culture. This means that one's understanding of national identity may have to change as a result of new circumstances in a given society. Hence, nation building is not a fixed, immutable process. Rather, it "is to reshape national identity to fit the existing characteristics of the society in question" (Fukuyama 2018: 141).

The kind of nation building that has taken place in the Nordic countries has undoubtedly been conducive to developing a wider radius of trust – meaning that inhabitants trust not only their family and neighbors (individuals they know), but also generally others elsewhere in society (individuals they do *not* know), and, notably, the country's public institutions. The wider question is whether this radius of trust can be developed and maintained in a more multicultural, multiethnic, and multireligious society.

The Nordic welfare state

In tracing the roots of the welfare state, should we look back to the Swedish vision of the *folkhem*, introduced in the 1930s? Or should we go back to the earliest public welfare arrangements of the late 1800s? Or must we go all the way back to Martin Luther and the Reformation in the early 1500s? If we deem this last and longest history to be the most valid, then we are claiming that religion was crucial to the Nordic version of the welfare state. In the academic world there is still strong disagreement on this point.

But whether the roots of the welfare state are buried in religious or secular historical soil, the Danish-American economist Henrik Fogh Rasmussen finds that the Nordic countries are romanticizing "Grundtvig, Stauning, and the *folkhem*". They do so at their peril, he says, because the Nordic welfare model is untenable in a globalized economy. As he advised in an article from 2011, "it is time to bid goodbye to the welfare state," which will become a millstone around the neck of the Nordic countries, threatening to draw them down into economic chaos. Instead of desperately struggling to save the remnants of a broken welfare state, the political leaders in the Nordic countries ought to strive to safely transition from the welfare state of the twentieth century to the "market state" of the twenty-first century. In Rasmussen's view, if the welfare state is not transformed into a market state, the Nordic societies will be overtaken and beaten in their attempt to compete with the new high-growth economies (Rasmussen 2011).

If this does happen, it will not only undermine the Nordic populations' feelings of belonging to a "people's home"; it will also influence the radical individualization which, according to the Swedish social scientists Henrik Berggren and Lars Trägårdh, now typifies the Nordic countries today. They believe the welfare state itself is the motor driving the individualization seen in the Nordic region, where, in recent decades, the individual has been set free from a variety of historically given relationships and social contexts at work, in family life, and in civil society.

Berggren and Trägårdh propose that the liberation of the individual has been the predominant aim of much political decision making regarding public welfare arrangements. The Nordic welfare model, they say, has had as its goals not just social security and economic solidarity, but also personal autonomy and individualization.

Although the path has not always been clear, throughout the twentieth century the welfare projects of the Nordic countries have pursued the ambition of liberating residents and citizens from many types of dependency: on family, on workplaces, and on civil organizations. The poor have been freed from their links to private charity, workers from employers, wives from husbands, children from parents, and aging parents from adult caregiving children. The goal has been not to socialize a country's economy, but to make its inhabitants autonomous.

Personal autonomy has been institutionalized through a wide variety of laws and policies that are pervasive and interconnected, affecting the relations and bonds between generations and genders. Interdependence among family members has been minimized with the individual taxation of spouses, while reforms in family law have all but removed a family's obligation to support its elderly. More or less universal daycare has made it possible for parents to work, and grant incomes paid to students independently of parental income have given young people a remarkable degree of independence from their families. Children and adolescents also enjoy a more independent status after corporal punishment was made illegal and the UN Convention on the Rights of the Child was adopted into law. Individuals have become less and less dependent on their families, but simultaneously more dependent on the state. A central aspect of this individual liberation consists in the relatively new and dramatically altered position and situation of female citizens. Following women's liberation, the individualization project put the whole pre-existing structure of social and bread-winning roles in the family under intense pressure (Berggren & Trägårdh 2011).

The big question is whether the dramatic turn that has taken place in the Nordic countries poses a threat to the welfare society – which, itself, gave birth to such an extreme degree of personal freedom and independence.

From a historical perspective, the liberation of the individual from social constraints and financial dependency on family, and in so many other respects, is a social and moral experiment on an enormous scale. So far it has largely succeeded, which is remarkable in itself. But can it continue to succeed? Or is it corroding the foundation of cultural, moral, and social capital on which its existence depends? We do not know for certain. So far, the process of radical individualization does not seem to have led to any widespread unraveling of the social fabric, and some findings indicate the exact opposite. In virtually all of the comparative international surveys conducted in recent years to measure happiness, trust, corruption, and other similar parameters, the Nordic countries exhibit some of the best scores – strongly suggesting that it is too early to reject the long-term viability of the Nordic model.

Chapter 10.
Conclusions

As demonstrated throughout this book, peoplehood is a complex concept that has undergone a series of transformations over the ages. From a Nordic and, more specifically, Scandinavian point of view, while it is true that for centuries or decades at a time there has been a broad consensus on one meaning, from time to time the word *folk* has taken on a new meaning.

For several centuries, the words "people" and "father" were twin concepts: no father without a people, and no people without a father. In hierarchic, patriarchal societies where the ruler was master and guardian - like those in the Nordic region - *folk* denoted individuals and groups who were subordinates or subjects.

The nobility and the clergy did not perceive themselves as part of "the people", which consisted of the lowest "estate" or class in Nordic societies: the peasantry. Martin Luther was a firm believer in patriarchal government - the rule of the *pater* or master - and his position is not surprising. Virtually all of his contemporaries subscribed to this view. Luther wrote his *Small Catechism* explicitly to teach the people to live as good Christians in a patriarchally governed society. The book became canonical, a mandatory textbook used for instruction and teaching, and for over

350 years it saturated and shaped the Nordic mentality. Learning and living by the *Small Catechism* became a prerequisite for anyone who wanted to live and interact in this type of community and society, which was organized in a rigid structure of classes and households.

Democracy is and always will be the alternative to patriarchal rule. Either the people as a body is ruled by a guardian and master, or the people governs itself. Either the people has power, or it is subjected to guardianship. This distinction is reflected in the shifting meaning of peoplehood, where the principal sense of *folk* changed from "subjects" to "sovereign body" in step with the political systems transitioning from patriarchal rule to democracy – government by the people.

The rise of the idea of democracy and the founding of nation-states from the late 1700s onwards gradually caused the older understanding of the word "people" to fade into the background. In its place, three main meanings crystallized: *folk* as a political concept; *folk* as a linguistic and cultural concept; and *folk* as a social concept. In the history of ideas, different thinkers represent these meanings: Jean-Jacques Rousseau the political; Johann Gottfried von Herder the linguistic and cultural; and Karl Marx and Friedrich Engels the social. These different understandings of "people" can support each other or undermine each other, depending on the context.

When democracy came resolutely knocking on Denmark's door in 1848, it intensified an already pressing and controversial question: Where should the border be drawn between "a Danish people" and "a German people"? Was it best drawn at the Elbe river, which was the border of the Danish state? Or should it be drawn along the Eider, thereby incorporating Schleswig into the Danish kingdom? Or was it best that it follow the Kongeå river, thereby surrendering Schleswig to Holstein and, by inference, to Germany? Or ought Schleswig be divided into two parts, one with

German people in it, and another with Danish people? The solution, in the first instance, was dictated in 1864 by Otto von Bismarck, who won the border war he waged on Denmark that year, leading to the incorporation of Holstein and Schleswig into Germany. In the second instance, as a consequence of World War I, the solution was to hold a referendum in Schleswig in 1920, the result of which brought the northern part of Schleswig "back home" to Denmark. The installation of democracy in Norway and Sweden did not have the same dramatic consequences as it did in Denmark. The main reason for this was that the other two Scandinavian countries did not have two large, co-existing languages, making them more homogeneous in that respect; the idea that "people" and "language" were synonymous concepts had serious consequences for the Danish state, precisely because it had two major languages, Danish and German.

During the 1800s the concept of peoplehood in the Nordic region was radically transformed. Early in that century a process began among new religious movements that were rebelling against the institution of the Lutheran state churches and, by extension, against the prevailing class system. These movements mainly involved peasants, domestic servants, and others of humble means. In the latter half of the 1800s the process of transformation was intensified by the struggle of the downtrodden rural class to gain political influence. The aims of the new religious movements, which grew from the bottom up, were to establish a sense of peoplehood and national identity, and to achieve self-government and self-management in civil society. In this context there are three outstanding figures in Scandinavia who merit special mention: N. F. S. Grundtvig in Denmark, Henrik Wergeland in Norway, and Erik Geijer in Sweden. Each in their own way, they made a decisive impact on the transformation of the Nordic countries by raising up the farmer as the core of "the people". This process was greatly advanced by the numerous "people's high schools" founded across the region. It is an unusual distinguishing feature of the political and societal aspects of "the Nordic way" that the groups who eventually developed into a better-educated rural class became largely liberal in their views and hence compatible with the principles of liberal democracy - which was definitely not the case in many other countries that tried to install various versions of democratic rule.

World War I clarified the labor movement's ideological foundation in the Nordic region. This was a contributing factor in transforming the region's social-democratic movements and parties from anti-national, class-based parties into broad people's parties. This led firstly to the rejection of the communist ideology's class-based understanding of the concept of "people", and secondly to the rejection of the national-socialists' (Nazis') race-based understanding of it. During the interwar years the foundation on which the activities of the social-minded democracies in Scandinavia were built consisted of a peaceful reform strategy resting on democratic principles. This process was supported by new worker's high schools and study circles.

The final transformation of the Scandinavian social-democratic parties from "class parties" to "people's parties" was achieved in the 1930s, under the leadership of three social-democratic prime ministers: Thorvald Stauning in Denmark, Johan Nygaardsvold in Norway, and Per Albin Hansson in Sweden. Each of the three countries would find its own way to reach a national compromise between "farmers" and "workers", which took place in 1933 in Denmark, in 1935 in Norway, and in 1936 in Sweden. This type of accord is unique to the Nordic region. The national compromises in Scandinavia laid the groundwork for what would gradually develop into the Nordic version of the welfare state, which is based on a combination of liberal *and* socialist principles. The formative and educational processes associated with this are intimately linked to the founding of the universal public school (in Denmark called *folkeskolen*) and the educating of new generations to revere democratic principles. Democracy was to be seen not merely as a form of government, but also as a way of life and a way of organizing a society – in the form of a welfare state. The leading ideologues in this process were the married couple Gunnar and Alva Myrdal in Sweden, and Hal Koch in Denmark.

As explained earlier, peoplehood is an elastic notion, and the word "people" has taken on new meanings from time to time. In the course of the 1800s, in the Scandinavian languages *folk* shifted from being a derogatory word to becoming a uniting rallying cry. Even after World War II, until around the mid-1960s, the *folk* concept was regarded, virtually as a matter of course, as the most basic constituent element of peoplehood for Danes, Norwegians, and Swedes. However, over recent decades the Nordic countries have all gradually become more diverse in terms of culture, ethnicity, and religion, and in step with the population's growing diversity, "peoplehood" is once again a topic of debate – not least in light of Europeanization, migration, and the viability of the welfare state.

"People" as a concept will surely take on new meanings in the years to come, as it has in the past, but *what* meanings it will encompass is hard to predict. The word itself will remain a battleground for a mix of contradicting and conflicting interests. Someday it may even be common for those living in the Nordic countries to speak about and perceive themselves as part of a "European people". Certainly no one owns or controls "people" as an idea, and throughout history the notion of peoplehood has worn many different guises. As for its future, that depends on our ideas of who, what, and where "the people" are.

Suggestions for further reading

Broadbridge, E. et al. (2011). *The School for Life. N. F. S. Grundtvig on Education for the People*. Aarhus University Press.

Campell, J. L., Hall, J. A., & Pedersen, O. K. (Eds.). (2008). *National Identity and the Varieties of Capitalism. The Danish Experience*. McGill Queen's University Press.

Hall, J. A., Korsgaard, O., & Pedersen, O. K. (Eds.). (2015). *Building the Nation. N. F. S. Grundtvig and Danish National Identity*. McGill Queen's University Press.

Jespersen, K. J. V. (2018). *A History of Denmark*. Red Globe Press.

Korsgaard, O. (2008). *The Struggle for the People. Five Hundred Years of Danish History in Short*. Aarhus University Press.

Árnason, J. P. & Wittrock, B. (Eds.). (2012). *Nordic Paths to Modernity*. Berghahn Books.

References

Adriansen, I. (1990). *Fædrelandet, folkeminderne og modersmålet*. Museumsrådet Sønderjylland.

Anderson, B. (1983). *Imagined Communities. Reflections on the Origin and Spread of* Nationalism. Verso Books.

Bente, F. & Dau, W.H.T. (1921). The Large Catechism by Martin Luther. In: *Triglot Concordia: The Symbolical Books of the Ev. Lutheran Church*. Concordia Publishing House. https://www.projectwittenberg.org/pub/resources/text/ wittenberg/luther/catechism/web/cat-01.html

Berggren, H. & Trägårdh, L. (2011). Social Trust and Radical Individualism. World Economic Forum.

Brandes, G. (1905). *Samlede Skrifter, 15*, 492. Gyldendalske Boghandels Forlag.

Broadbridge, E. (2015). *Living Wellsprings. The Hymns, Songs and Poems of N.F.S. Grundtvig.* Aarhus University Press.

Broadbridge, E. & Korsgaard, O. (2019). *The Common Good. N. F. S. Grundtvig as Politician and Contemporary Historian.* Aarhus University Press.

Bryld, C. (1992). *Den demokratiske socialismes gennembrudsår.* Selskabet til Forskning i Arbejderbevægelsens Historie.

Christiansen, N. F. (2007). Velfærdsstaten og det nationale. In J. Petersen, K. Petersen, & L. Petersen (Eds.), *13 værdier bag den danske velfærdsstat.* Syddansk Universitetsforlag.

Dahl, R. A. (1991). *Democracy and its Crisis.* Yale University Press.

Duedahl, P. (2007). *Fra overmenneske til UNESCO-menneske.* Aalborg Universitet.

Elias, N. & Habermas, J. (1994). Nasjonalisme og nasjonal identitet. *Cappelens upopulære skrifter, 19.*

Engels, F. (1848). *Neue Rheinische Zeitung, 99.* Clouth.

Engelstoft, L. (1808). *Tanker om Nationalopdragelsen.* Gyldendal.

Frisch, H. (1933). *Pest over Europa.* Henrik Koppels Forlag.

Fukuyama, F. (2014). *Political Order and Political Decay.* Profile Books.

Fukuyama, F. (2015). Nation Building and State Building. In J. A. Hall, O. Korsgaard, & O. K. Pedersen (Eds.), *Building the Nation: N. F. S. Grundtvig and Danish National Identity.* McGill-Queen's University Press.

Fukuyama, F. (2018). *Identity: Contemporary identity politics and the struggle for recognition.* Profile Books.

Glenthøj, R. & Ottosen, M. N. (2021). *Union eller undergang: Kampen for et forenet Skandinavien.* Gads Forlag.

Greenfeld, L. (1992). *Nationalism. Five roads to Modernity.* Harvard University Press.

Grundtvig, N. F. S. (1905). Verdens Krønike 1812. In *Udvalgte Skrifter* (Vol. 2). Gyldendal.

Grundtvig, N. F. S. (1909). Dansk Rigsdags-Tale imod den
saakaldte 'almindelige Værnepligt'. In *Udvalgte Skrifter*
(Vol. 9). Gyldendal.

Götz, A. (2005). *Hitlers Volksstaat. - Raub, Rassenkrieg und
nationaler Sozialismus*. Fischer S. Verlag.

Historiegruppen. (1950). *Danmarks Historie*. Det danske Forlag.

Hitler, A. (2002). *Mein Kampf*. Translated into English by
James Murphy. Project Gutenberg of Australia. https://
gutenberg.net.au/ebooks02/0200601.txt

Ilsøe, H. (1991). Danskerne og deres fædreland. In O. Feldbæk
(Ed.), *Dansk identitetshistorie* (Vol. 1). C.A. Reitzel.

Israel, J. (2010). *A Revolution of the Mind*. Princeton University
Press.

Koch, H. (1942). *Dagen og Vejen*. Westermann.

Koch, H. (1945). *Hvad er demokrati?* Gyldendal.

Koch, H. (1966). Ordet eller sværdet. (Two chronicles from
Berlinske Aftenavis, September 12 and 19, 1945). In *Om
tolerance*. Gyldendal.

Kofoed-Hansen, H. P. (1869). *Et folk - Folket: Bidrag til
Demotheismens Charakteristik*. Andr. Fred. Høst (Høst &
Søn).

Korsgaard, O. (2008). How to Establish the Nation in the Hearts
of the People. In Campbell, C. et al., *National Identity
and the Varieties of Capitalism. The Danish Experience*.
McGill-Queen's University Press.

Korsgaard, O. (2014). *N.F.S. Grundtvig - as a Political Thinker*.
DJØF Publishing.

Korsgaard, O. (2019). *A foray into Folk High School Ideology*.
FFD's Forlag.

Lundgreen-Nielsen, F. (1992). Grundtvig og danskhed. In O.
Feldbæk (Ed.), *Dansk identitetshistorie* (Vol. 3). C.A.
Reitzel.

Mann, M. (2012). *Fascists*. Cambridge University Press.

Marx, K. & Engels, F. (1888). *Manifesto of the Communist Party*.
Translated into English by Samuel Moore. http://www.
yorku.ca/comninel/courses/4090pdf/manifest.pdf

McLuhan, M. (1964). *Understanding Media: The Extensions of Man*. New York, McGraw-Hill.

Müller, J.-W. (2011). *Contesting Democracy*. Yale University Press.

Myrdal, A. (1940). *Nation and Family*. M.I.T. Press.

Myrdal, A. & Myrdal G. (1946). *Kontakt med Amerika*. Athenæum.

Nielsen, J. (1971). *Demokratiet og krigen. En undersøgelse af samspillet mellem demokrati, nationalisme og krigsførelse*. Wøldike.

Nielsen, J. (1987). *1864. Da Europa gik af lave*. Odense Universitetsforlag.

Nissen, H. & Poulsen, H. (1963). *På dansk friheds grund*. Gyldendal.

Elias, N. & Habermas, J. (1974). Nasjonalisme og nasjonal identitet. *Cappelens upopulære skrifter, 19*.

Petersen, N. (1984). *Kultusministeriet: Organisation og arkiv, 21*.

Rasmussen, H. F. (2011). Det er på tide at sige farvel til velfærdsstaten. *Information*, August 6–7.

Schuyler, R. L. (1929). *Parliament and the British Empire*. Columbia University Press.

Smith, A. D. (2015). Icons of Nationalism. In J. A. Hall, O. Korsgaard, & O. K. Pedersen (Eds.), *Building the Nation: N. F. S. Grundtvig and Danish National Identity*. McGill-Queen's University Press.

Smith, R. E. (1994). *Luther's Little Instruction Book*. The Small Catechism by Martin Luther. https://www.projectwittenberg.org/pub/resoúrces/text/wittenberg/luther/little.book/book-1.txt

Sørensen, H. P. (1943). *F. J. Borgbjerg*. Forlaget Fremad.

Tilton, T. (1991). *The Political Theory of Swedish Social Democracy: Through the Welfare State to Socialism*. Clarendon Press.

Zernatto, G. (1944). The History of a Word. *The Review of Politics, 6*(3), 351–366. Cambridge University Press.